NARROW IS THE WAY

Embracing the True Way into Life

JAY R. LEACH

Order this book online at www.trafford.com
or email orders@trafford.com

Most Trafford titles are also available at major online book retailers.

Cover By: Magdalene J. Leach

Printed in the United States of America.

ISBN: 978-1-4907-3937-3 (sc)
ISBN: 978-1-4907-3939-7 (hc)
ISBN: 978-1-4907-3938-0 (e)

Library of Congress Control Number: 2014910723

Trafford rev. 06/13/2014

 www.trafford.com

North America & international
toll-free: 1 888 232 4444 (USA & Canada)
fax: 812 355 4082

CONTENTS

BOOKS BY JAY R. LEACH

How Should We Then Live

Behold the Man

The Blood Runs Through It

Drawn Away

Give Me Jesus

A Light unto My Path

Grace that Saves

Narrow Is the Way

THIS BOOK IS DEDICATED

TO
OUR PRECIOUS LORD
AND
SAVIOR, JESUS CHRIST

ONE SOLITARY LIFE

He was born in an obscure village, the child of a peasant woman. He grew up in still another village, where He worked in a carpenter shop until He was 30. Then for three years He was an itinerant preacher. He never wrote a book. He never held an office. He never had a family or owned a house. He didn't go to college. He never traveled more than 200 miles from the place He was born. He did none of the things one usually associates with greatness. He had no credentials but Himself. He was only 33 when public opinion turned against Him. His friends deserted Him. He was turned over to His enemies and went through the mockery of a trial. He was nailed to a cross between two thieves when He was dead He was laid in a borrowed grave through the pity of a friend. Nineteen centuries have come and gone, and today He is the central figure of the human race, the leader of mankind's progress. All the armies that ever marched, all the navies that ever sailed, all the parliaments that ever sat, all the kings that ever reigned, put together, have not affected the life of man on earth as much as that One Solitary Life. "Do You Know Who He Is?"[1]

By: Dr. James Allen Francis in "The Real Jesus and Other Sermons" 1925

INTRODUCTION

Twentieth century America seems to have been marked by people who claimed their own personal demons; and science and reason replaced God's revelation as master of the culture. The twenty-first century seems to be marked by people with their own personal Gods: Christianity's God of Creation or secular humanism's god of self. Thus, we have the two ways to life, human wisdom and truth versus God's wisdom and true truth. Some churches attempt concepts of doing church that involve both. But God, the Creator, will have no other God before Him!

Times have changed! There is a historical shift in the culture and churches today. In the midst of this shift many of God's people are confused and *losing their way*. The biblical consensus in America has all but been wiped out by a humanistic consensus forged by secular humanism and what I call, a religious Christianity of many gods. Sadly, both are tools of the spirit of this world focused on derailing this great fount of grace. Notice the progress Satan is making with his plans to annihilate the biblical family and marriage of one man and one woman using abortions, same sex marriages, cohabitation, multi-divorces and multi-marriages.

America has been God's main depository of Christianity for the past three hundred years. Therefore, we should know better than most, no matter how often the people of a society decide to change their philosophies of life, and their religions [to serve multicultural gods], God's narrow way for the true children of God remains unchanging.

Today, the slightest opposition to faith often causes many who profess to be Christians to abandon their allegiance to Christ and His church. **God's narrow way** is our obedience to His will, His infallible Word in Christ, and His immutable way. In Matthew 7:13-14, Jesus said,

7

*"Enter by the narrow gate; for wide is the gate and broad is the way that leads to destruction, and there are many who go in by it. Because **narrow is the gate** and **difficult** is the **way** which lends to life, and there are **few** who find it."*

He continually emphasized the difficulty in following Him. Contributing to this, Jesus added that there will be many false prophets and teachers misleading the multitudes, including many who formerly professed faith in Christ. Demonically inspired, they give the people what they really want: entertainment, a *sense* of escape, hope and purpose when times become difficult for them. Lacking true biblical knowledge and spiritual life – many Christians are living like pagans accepting their difficulties as judgment or they accept them as something to be tolerated as a normal part of life.

Jesus emphasized the **difficulty** in following Him. For the past thirty or forty years Satan through secular humanism's (atheism) and religious Christianity's (legalism) has really accelerated the spreading of their erroneous philosophies. This has resulted in the vanishing of our biblical worldview, morals and values, as *wickedness* and *lawlessness increases at an alarming rate* (see Matthew 24:12). Love and trust has become evasive to the average person as a result of the extreme lawlessness in the society today; and it is seriously beginning to affect many in the Christian community. What makes Jesus' prediction even more difficult to believe is that many Christians ignore the fact that the world already dislikes Christians and their God. Certainly Satan wants to keep the people in darkness. Something comes before and after the passage of Scripture where Jesus said, "Ask and it shall be given unto you." Salvation! Which is by grace alone through faith alone is not optional. It calls for:

- Hearing – the Gospel of Christ – (believe the Gospel to the saving of your soul).
- Repenting – (Receive the Gospel, turn and agree with the truths of God's Word concerning His eternal plan for you).
- Submitting to Christ as Lord – (give yourself wholly to Him as Lord of every area of life).
- Willing – (to walk in obedience to: His Will, His Word and His Way).

Again, in Matthew 19:16-23, Jesus engaged in a conversation with a rich young ruler, who asked Him, the requirements for gaining eternal life. Before answering the question, Jesus wanted to impress upon him:

• The high standard required by God and,
• The absolute futility of seeking salvation through one's own merit (Col. 1:13-14).

Unlike the disciples' response in (v. 25), seeing the impossibility of keeping the Law exclaimed, *"Who then can be saved?"* This young man confidently declared that he was qualified for heaven under those terms. The test came in verse 21, when Jesus finally answered his question, He bid the young man, *"Go sell what you have and give to the poor....... and come, follow Me."* The young man failed the test! It probably never entered his mind that Christ must be first in our lives. Because of his love for material things which became a stumbling block or idol; he *rejected* Jesus' claim for his life. Our last glimpse of him is his walking away in unbelief. In this discourse, Jesus was underscoring the impossibility for anyone's being saved by their own works or merit.

Since Adam and Eve's fall in the Garden of Eden; this has been Satan's **great deception** for humankind. Many people are deceived today with thinking that they can by-pass God's Will, His Word and His Way through their own works or merit. Satan has kept that same deceptive lie out there before our eyes through the centuries. Many think that fortune and wealth equate to God's grace; and is therefore deemed proof of God's approval. They normally give more thinking that it makes them more likely candidates for heaven [religious Christianity]. There is an abundant life promised in the Scripture for those who are willing to choose "the narrow way."

In choosing this life, we must be righteous and ready as the church to do as Jesus has commanded us to do: **"Make disciples** as you go, **baptize them** in the name of the Father, Son and the Holy Spirit; and **teach them** to do everything that I commanded you" (see Matthew 28:19-20). This commitment also includes **social justice.** The failure of the church and individual Christians is due to striving to do supernatural work in the natural! Only the outpouring of the Holy Spirit's power will enable us to make a difference. That is the "Narrow Way."

The promise of this divine enablement is Acts 1:8 was the last thing Jesus said before He ascended. Like His disciples this word should keep ringing in our ears: *You will receive power ...... You will be My witnesses ...... You will receive power .... You will be My witnesses.* Our Lord promised to supernaturally equip them and us to establish His kingdom in Judea, Jerusalem, and Samaria, and to the ends of the earth, [our part].

We have no excuse. Another reason for failure on our part is the results of individuals and local churches moving away from [The Event of the cross and resurrection] and Great Commandments, our first love (see Matthew 22:37-39).

Jesus said, "You shall love the Lord your God with all your heart, with all your soul and with all your mind. "You shall love your neighbor as yourself." The believer's whole moral duty and motivation for Christian living are summed up in these two commandments: love for God and love for one's neighbors. It is every Christians' duty to **evangelize** those out of the arc of safety.

Satan is drawing people very subtly to compromise with the sins of men and women knowing that they are in violation of God's moral law as their right! Human affections and sympathy toward the sinner and their sins take priority – over God's Word, His will and His way. More and more people including many Christians are being assimilated into a non-biblical secular humanistic worldview as a result of their dedication to science and rational thinking [reason].

The great preacher Charles Spurgeon admitted, "Without the Spirit of God we can do nothing. We are like ships without wind or chariots without steeds. Like branches with out sap, we are withered. Like coals without fire, we are useless."[2]

These Christians have reverted to the (bondage) of law and legalism; **while their atheistic counterpart seeks to silence or do away with God's moral Law. In many cases the Christian knows that to do so is error by choice. Embrace the narrow way with its correct beliefs and Christian living.** We are promised in Daniel 11:32, *"But the people who know their God shall be strong, and carry out great exploits."*

Jay R. Leach
.Fayetteville, NC

SECTION I
THE WAY INTO LIFE

CHAPTER 1

JESUS IS LORD

Sometime ago I read an article concerning the handling of counterfeit money by the U.S. Treasury Department. It stated emphatically, "The only thing they do with counterfeit money is burn it!" The article then explains that their trainees study the real money so thoroughly, that a counterfeit bill would immediately be detected by their thoroughly trained sight and feel.

Similarly, an exhaustive examination of the early church from its inception will enable us to easily identify religious Christianity's non-biblical church concepts practiced by many in today's postmodern world.

We cannot compare

In a postmodern world the rational arguments for the existence of God are cold and lifeless. However, a community of people gladly considers it a blessing to be defined by God's salvation event in Jesus Christ; and becomes Spirit-formed as true and living examples of a local and universal *oneness*. Thus, reflecting volumes to the world about [the Calvary event] and the saving grace of Christ that dwells within us.

The distinguishing characteristic of allowing ourselves to be defined this way is the restoration of a *supernatural experience* in the church, seen and unseen. The philosophical *shift* of the postmodern world from reason to the mystery or supernatural view provides a rich cultural context for the restoration of the early or first century view of the faith and the *finished* work of Christ. Therefore, it is in all sincerity not feasible to attempt comparing the life of Christ followers [Christians] with the principals and practices of secular humanism and religious Christianity, both will be covered thoroughly in a later section.

This approach to the "supernatural experience" is the strongest reality of God's presence to a lost world,

The Church throughout History

The Early Church	The Institutional Church	The Reformation Church
[PURITY]	**[APOSTATE]**	**[RESTORATION]**
Pentecost – A.D. 391	A.D. 391 – A.D. 1517	A.D. 1517 – Present
Unity in the body Christ (John 17:21; Ephesians 4:11-13)	of Sacramental/ Judicial (Rev. 2-3)	Unity in the body of body of Christ (Rev. 3)[3]

The Early Church

The church throughout its history has appeared in many different cultures and therefore no one expression of the church stands alone as the true visible body of Christ. A goal for the body of Christ in the postmodern world is to accept diversity as a restoration reality, and at the same time seek unity in the process. The idea being common ground for the various forms of the true church – all based on its being one, holy and apostolic in teaching and authority.

One way of accomplishing this unity is the view that there is only *one* church, but it is expressed in many cultural ways. Jesus expressed His desire for the oneness of the church in the words of His prayer that, "all of them may be one ……. That the world may believe that You sent Me" (John 17:21). In the early church Jesus' statement meant *"visible unity."*

Concerning the oneness of the church, the Apostle Paul exhorts, *"for by One Spirit we were all baptized into one body; whether Jews or Greeks, whether slaves or free; and all made to drink into one Spirit"* (I Corinthians 12:1-3). In Ephesians 4:3, he counsels, the church should be, *"eager to maintain the unity of the Spirit in the bond of peace."* I pray that the leadership of the churches realize the degree to which secular humanism and religious Christianity are allowed to reign in churches is the degree to which the Holy Spirit is hindered in making those churches effective. Thus, their fundamental character of holiness, universal and apostolic kingdom service is impeded. This is depicted in the diagram above:

- The early Church was marked by its purity – Unity fueled by persecution.
- The Church of the Middle Ages or Dark Ages was marked by its apostate condition – "falling away" from the truths of God's Word.
- The Reformation Church is marked by restoration of biblical truths lost during the pre and Middle Ages and unity in the body of Christ through truths of God's Word.

Holiness

Many Christians are hindered in their walk over the issue of the church's holiness. The church is admonished to, *"Be holy, because I am holy"* (see 1 Peter 1:16). Contrary to many forms and practices this passage should be understood individually as well as standing for the whole body of Christ, for Peter defined the church as *"a chosen people, a royal priesthood, a holy nation, a people belonging to God"* (1 Peter 2:9). In studying the New Testament, we quickly become aware that the visible church contains both the clean and the unclean; as is indicated in Jesus' parable of the wheat and the tares. Thus, the visible church contains both saints and sinners [truth and counter-truth]. The church on earth then may be regarded as having a church within the church. The church that is "holy and blameless," without "spot or wrinkle," is the one Christ, the Son will present to the Father.

Denominations are realizing that the old separatist model of "my way or the highway" is for all practical kingdom purposes – out! Additionally we are finding that we must be more tolerant of the human weaknesses of the church. For example I was at one time convinced that my concept of Christianity was the right one and my church was correct in its views. Therefore I would not associate with some churches that I believed had a lot of wrong views. Then one day I discovered that the church is not yet perfect (ethically nor doctrinally). Now I am able to embrace the entire body of Christ. This affirmation that the church is universal [all over the world] enables me to feel at home with other Protestant churches as we labor together to restore *the faith* of the early church. The faith based on the solid foundation of apostolic doctrine, first delivered to the saints (see Jude 3).

Christianity is the only major faith to have as its
central event the humiliation of its God.

Believer's sing,

"Dear dying Lamb,"
"thy precious Blood
Shall never lose its power,
Till all the ransomed Church of God
Be saved to sin no more."

Catholic

The word catholic was first used by Ignatius when he wrote, "Wherever Jesus Christ is, there is the Catholic Church." By this designation he pointed to the fullness of truth: the church that is catholic has all the truth – Jesus Christ.[4] This catholic is not to be confused with the Roman Catholic Church. The early church used the word catholic to mean universal.

The catholic or universal vision of early Christians was evident in the impact of the gospel as it rapidly expanded for the first three centuries. The majority of the new converts were simple, humble people: slaves, women, and soldiers. It has been suggested that this existed due to the fact that most of the population were in that class. History records that by the end of the second century many people with the sharpest minds of the day were becoming Christ followers.

People turned to Christ in the second century, as they do today, for various reasons. Some prominent factors, however, worked upon the minds of humankind; and appear to have contributed to the growth of Christianity:

- First, early Christians were moved by a burning conviction. The Event had taken place. God invaded time, and humankind had been redeemed.
- Second, the Gospel of Christ met a widely felt need in the hearts of people. The early Christians realized by grace that only the active love of God – rather than the individual's natural love could make the Christian life possible and direct the believer outward to the needs of others.
- Third, the practical expression of Christian love was among the most powerful causes of Christian success. The pagans remarked, "See how these Christians loved one another."[5]
- Early Christian love found expression in the care of the poor, of widows and orphans; in visiting those in prison, and those condemned to death in the mines; and in acts of compassion during famine, earthquake, or war.
- Christian faith had especially advanced through the loving service rendered to strangers, and their care for the burial of the dead.
- Finally, *persecution* in many instances helped to publicize the Christian faith.

For these and many other reasons the Christian churches multiplied until Rome could neither ignore nor suppress the faith. It finally had to come to terms with it. There are a number of cases of the conversion of pagans in the very moment of witnessing the condemnation and deaths of Christians. This period of persecution was marked by the Christians' joyful acceptance of suffering as the way appointed by the Lord to lead His heavenly kingdom.

People always view with suspicion those persons who are different. Conformity not distinctiveness is the way to a trouble-free life. Thus, by simply living according to Jesus' teachings, the Christian is a *constant unspoken condemnation* of the pagan way of life. The early Christians were authentic followers of the narrow way. Not going about criticizing, condemning and disapproving, nor were they consciously self-righteous and superior as the counterfeits often portray. They reject the *narrow way* of living.

One down-fall of many Christians today is to talk a lot about what they **are** biblically, but their lifestyle or what they **do** does not coincide.

That must change if we are going to be **salt** and **light** to the postmodern society, where many people are earnestly seeking true reality.[6]

Fundamental to the Christian life-style and the cause
of endless hostility was the Christian's rejection of the
pagan gods. How do we measure up today?

The Greeks and Romans had gods for every aspect of living:

- For sowing and reaping
- For rain and wind
- For volcanoes and rivers
- For birth and death

But to the Christians these gods were nothing – and their denial of them **marked** them as *"enemies of the human race."* A person could not simply reject the gods without arousing scorn as a social misfit:

- Every pagan's meal began with a liquid offering and prayer to the pagan gods. A Christian could not share in that.
- Most pagan feasts and social parties were held within the perimeter of the temple and after the sacrifice was made, the invitation was usually to dine "at the table" of some god. A Christian could not attend such feasts.
- When the Christian refused the invitation to some social occasion, he or she was considered rude, boorish, and discourteous.

The Christians' fear of idolatry also led to problems in making a living [in the market place].

- A brick mason might be involved in building the walls of a pagan temple.
- A tailor may be involved in making robes for a heathen priest.
- An incense-maker may be making incense for the pagan sacrifices.

- Unlike his pagan neighbor the Christian refused to take his weak and unwanted children out in the woods and leave them to die or be picked up by robbers.
- This regard for life also applied to sex and marriage.

This widespread hatred of Christians resulted in the first persecution from the Romans in A.D. 64. It was probably during this persecution that Peter and Paul suffered martyrdom in Rome. The fact was, the Christian as a Christian was legally an outlaw. "Public hatred," says Tertullian, "asks but one thing, **not** the investigation of the crimes charged, **but** simply the confession of the Christian name."

In his book, *Church History in Plain Language,* Dr. Bruce Shelly enlightens us. The supreme cause of Roman persecution of Christians arose from the tradition of emperor worship. This conflict between Christ and Caesar was gradual in coming:

- The worship of the Emperor assumed central place in the life of the empire
- The Roman Empire built a system of roads which were cleared of robbers,
- The seas were clear of pirates, *a new security* entered into life of the people.

This was called the "Roman peace," which resulted in a deep and heartfelt gratitude to the spirit of Rome. The Roman Empire was comprised of many different languages, cultures, faiths and traditions; which imposed a problem for unification.[7]

There is no unifying force like the force of a common religion – nor is there greater disunity as experienced without a common religion!

It was an easy step for the spirit of Rome to become the goddess of Roma. By the second century B.C. there were many temples in Asia Minor to the goddess of Roma. People need a symbol; so the spirit of Rome and the goddess of Roma were incarnated in the emperor. There is no unifying force like the force of a common religion; nor is there greater disunity as experienced without a common religion. As a result Caesar worship became "the keystone" of imperial policy. It was *deliberately organized* in every province in the empire. Satan is using this strategy to try to eradicate Christianity from America by offering multi-cultures and multi-religions to nullify the unity and consensus of biblical Christianity. Christianity is a living organism [*a life*] which requires a birth, life, and growth (see John 3:3, 16).

Unlike Christianity, religion is actually an organization which *relies* upon obedience to established laws and rules of men [in most cases, dead men]. Christianity is life in Christ, the living founder! Only those who have experienced the new birth through Jesus Christ are authentic Christians. There is a religious Christianity, [counterfeit], as I have explained in an earlier section; which is one of Satan's major weapons used in his attempt to derail the Church of God through a web of customs, laws, and manmade traditions.

Notice, everywhere in the Empire temples to the godhead of the emperor appeared. Very subtly people within the empire came to believe that any allegiance in conflict with loyalty to the emperor and therefore to the empire, would only lead to disintegration of order.[8]

Thus, Christian worship and Caesar worship met head-on:

The one thing no Christian would ever say was: "Caesar is Lord."

For the Christian, Jesus Christ and He alone was Lord. To the Roman the Christian seemed utterly *intolerant* and *insanely stubborn:* worse he or she was a self-confessed disloyal citizen.

Thus the familiar affirmation "Jesus is Lord," now almost a Christian cliché, originally challenged the lordship of the Roman Empire. It still does. The Lordship of Christ versus the lordship of the empire is the same contrast, as the opposition that we see in the Kingdom of God versus the kingdom of this world.

The body of Christ must prepare our saints for the ever-increasing battle as more and more secular judges are appointed to the bench. We must be able to counter this secular assault with saints not only in the courts but throughout the marketplace.

Had the Christians been willing to burn that pinch of incense and say formally, "Caesar is Lord," they could have gone on worshipping Christ to their hearts content – but the true Christians would not compromise![9]

Rome regarded them as a band of potential revolutionaries threatening the very existence of the empire. Thus, we see that Caesar worship was primarily a test of *political loyalty* between the praises Christians offered in worship and the adulation Roman citizens directed to the reigning emperor.

It happened in the Roman Empire. Do we think America is exempt? Everywhere in this country we are seeing this principle being applied through a movement that among other things claims you can be a Christian and still embrace another faith or religion. One such group has named this union Chrislam; which fosters an "Islamized gospel." This concept allows the Muslim to become a Christian while continuing the practice of Islam.[10] Yoga and other Eastern practices have been assimilated by many Christians. Use of the word "karma" has quickly become American slang. When ignored history has a tendency to repeat itself!

The Revelation of John reflects the Christian response to the imperial cult in Asia Minor toward the end of the first century. John traces the oppression of believers to the devil himself, to the great dragon, who wages war against the saints *today* through two agents – the spirits of the beasts of Revelation 13:

- The first is the beast from the sea (or abyss), the imperial power – Antichrist.
- The second is the beast from the land, the imperial worship – the false prophet.

And what was the Christians' defense against this deadly attack from Rome? They conquered the dragon, John says, *"by the blood of the Lamb and by the word of their testimony, for they loved not their lives even unto death"* (Revelation 12:11).[11]

I will cover the two beast and today's church in the next chapter. Again the church is catholic or continuous. We are a part of the apostolic body of Christ; which was born on the streets of Jerusalem on the Day of Pentecost and continues building to this day. Remember, the full meaning of the word *catholic* may be defined by such words as "universal," "identical," "orthodox," "continuous," and "wholeness or fullness."

- The church is **universal** not only in the sense that it is worldwide, but also in the sense that it is *grounded* in the universality of the atonement [the "finished work of Christ"].
- The church is **identical** in that it always remains true to itself in history.
- The church is always to remain **orthodox** [established doctrine].

To identify with catholicity, then, is to believe in the continuity of Christ's work in history and to affirm the whole faith, as we restore the faith of the early Christians, a faith based on solid content of God's Word.

Apostolic

The concept of the apostolic restores by Christ's authority and sovereignty, His spiritual "gifts" to the church: apostles, prophets, evangelists, pastors, and teachers (see Ephesians 4:11). For the specific purpose of equipping the saints for the work of ministry, for the edifying of the body of Christ, **till we all come into the unity of the faith** and of the **knowledge** of the Son of God, to a perfect man, to the measure of the stature of the fullness of Christ; that we should no longer be children, tossed to and fro and carried about with every wind of doctrine, by the trickery of men, in the cunning craftiness of deceitful plotting, but, speaking the truth in love, may grow up in all things into Him who is, the Head – Christ – from whom the whole body, joined and knit by what every joint supplies, according to the effective working by which every part does its share, causes growth of the body for the edifying of itself in love (see Ephesians 2:1-10; 4:12-16).

These "gifts of men" Christ gave to the body of Christ [were given **until?**] Emphasis added throughout. More and more church leaders are coming to grips with the realization that for the church to be apostolic, **all** of the spiritual gifts that were present in the early church should be recognized and exercised by the church today [Study Ephesians 2:20; 1Corinthians 12-14; Romans 12]. In fact their functions never ceased to be practiced though many individuals substituted secular titles such as superintendent, overseer and others instead of the apostolic language. The restoration of apostolic language will be a uniting rather than a dividing factor. Thus the whole body of Christ shares in the apostolic faith handed down in the life of the church through the centuries (see Ephesians 4:7).

My argument is that the postmodern world in turning from science and reason to mystery presents a rich cultural context for the restoration of the early church's supernatural view of the complete body of Christ, the Church (universal). This includes the redemptive plan and work of **God**, the Father, the finished work of **Christ,** the Son and His continued presence in and to the world through the work and ministry of the **Holy Spirit** in the saints. The Lord promised us power after the Holy Spirit has come upon us (see Acts 1:8). Through Christ we can be a **powerful** countering force against Satan's humanistic and religious false teachers' attacks on:

- The moral law of God [the truths of God's Word]
- The things of God [the institutions of God, true worship, marriage and family, government, and revealed knowledge]
- The people of God [true saints]
- The man and woman of God [discerners of deception]

Christ has not changed His mind; He is still coming back for a church without spot or wrinkle. If not countered we will soon face right here in America *[as is already happening in some other parts of the world]* some of the same types of persecution as did the saints of the early church. Shelly reports, Christians were:

- Ostracized
- Denied employment because of their faith
- Hated for being Christ followers
- Crucified
- Fed to the lions
- Sewn up in the skins of wild beasts; then large dogs were let loose on them and they were torn to pieces.
- Tied to mad bulls and dragged to death

- Burned at the stake in Nero's garden – while he and his friends enjoyed the horrible spectacles to the fullest.[12]

These barbaric and cruel acts only reinforce, Jesus' warning to us that without Him man will do anything. While the church sleeps secular humanism marches on:

- In 1963 – the Bible and prayer were banned from the school.
- In 1973 – abortions became legal; and since then 155 million babies have been aborted – January 22, 2014, marked the 41st anniversary of Roe vs. Wade.
- In 2013 – Same sex marriages and cohabitation became legal in many States.

Fifty years ago these things were unheard of above a whisper; however today they are very subtly becoming cultural norms. Satan is gradually working his destructive plan against this nation. With the stroke of a pen powerful atheistic federal judges can take away the fundamental rights of individual citizens. It is happening today with state and community populations. For example several judges in three or four different states recently struck down State Constitutional amendments banning same sex marriages as approved by the majority vote of the people. "We the people" is very subtly being forced out!

I believe that Satan's special targets today are those men and women who are truly committed to preaching, teaching and living as salt and light – through the power of the Holy Spirit and the *truths* of God's Word. I want to emphasize my purpose from beginning to the end is to emphasize the importance of evangelism, nurture and social justice [helping men, women, girls and boys come to know Christ as Savior and Lord and grow on to maturity] through the need:

- To walk daily with the Lord
- To study and meditate on God's Word
- To live a life of prayer
- To show forth the love, compassion, and holiness of our Lord
- Fortify yourself in the Lord and His Word in preparation for Satan's onslaught of the saints in our time!

I emphasize equally the need for us to live this out openly in every area of culture and life.

For Example

The direction of a society is determined by its world view. From what I have reported so far in this chapter, it should be obvious, where our nation is heading under its adopted humanistic worldview. I believe we can see from God's point of view what happens to any nation that forgets Him. Notice these verses found in II Chronicles 15, talking about ancient Israel:

And for many days Israel was *without the true God* and *without a teaching priest* and *without law*.......... And in those times there was no peace to him who went out or to him who came in, for many disturbances afflicted all the inhabitants of the lands. And nation was crushed by nation, and city by city, *for God troubled them with every kind of distress* (vv. 3, 5-6).

A survey of these verses reveals a picture of what great spiritual and social chaos happens when a society breaks down. Three essentials necessary for national life were missing in Israel – I believe the three of them are on the verge of becoming missing in American life today:

The true God

The first essential missing was the true God. The writer did not say that the Israelites turned to atheists or no longer believed in God. From all appearances everything at the temple was going on as usual. The people were present and the sacrificial fires were still burning. However, Israel no longer had a correct view of God, and accordingly they were no longer accomplishing His will for them.

Like so many today in our society, they wanted a convenient God, one who would react to their beckoning. A God they could control. In other words they wanted to be god. Any god you can control isn't the *true* God. They wanted God to adjust to their whims. You adjust to God.

The Israelites did not want the true God directing their national life, reminding them of the narrow way that He had planned for them. They wanted to pursue their own personal interests and desires. Our American culture doesn't care for a God like that either. From all indications a great number of churches aren't very interested in the true God either, because He would cramp their lifestyles and pleasures. When the people of God act this way they are foregoing any kind of true representation of the true and living God.

The teaching priest

The second essential missing was the teaching priest. First of all notice, the verse does not say they had no priests. But the priests had ceased teaching the truth of God's Word. They had traded revelation for entertainment. Worship had evolved into the equivalent of a social club meeting. The temple was no longer the center of all life and conscience of the culture nor did they convince people to consider the true God any longer.

Another thing they did that's very prevalent in churches today was to allow emotions to replace truth. Israel suffered the absence of spiritual leaders who took the authority of Scripture for all of life.

When people do not have truth they do not have anything to prick their hearts when they make wrong choices. They become *"seared in their own conscience as a branding iron"* (1Timothy 4:2). It is as if people are inoculated against "the right way." A mark of postmodernism is, people want certainty in the every day important things – but without having to admit that there is an available body of truth, the Holy Bible. So relativism, the new tolerance and political correctness rule the society.

What use to happen to young people leaving home for college, the military or some other endeavor that put them on their own is now happening many years earlier, for a variety of reasons. The main reason being children are now faced with the multicultural atheistic curriculum in all learning institutions beginning with pre-school. Soon few will be around who remember when the "absolutes" were believed in the culture and taught in schools. Today, children are taught early on by parents and significant others, "There are no absolutes!" So where do we find true truth? By the time our children reach high school they have been fully indoctrinated that:

- One person's answers and ideas are just as good as anyone else's.

- Everybody's answers are right so nobody is right.
- When the society has lost truth, there is no meaning, because people are no longer really sure about anything.

So where do we find truth?

God's Law

The third missing essential in Israel was God's law. When the culture has a false view of the reality of the true God built on Satan's deceptive information – God begins to remove the restraints of His law, and evil grows unrestrictedly. What we see around us is the ever-increasing evil as God's restraints are loosened. The rapid deterioration of our culture all over America is that reality. Some of the countries that we once characterized as third world or underdeveloped have come into their own through the mighty Holy Spirit led revivals; and are now sending their missionaries to evangelize America and other Western nations.

The Scripture states there are things that even pagans would not do out of fear or respect for God. But once God is removed from the culture or pushed to the margin as He is today in our society – then the truth standard for the society is gone. God becomes your worst enemy. That's what happened to Israel.

At the time Asa was king of Judah. Remember the nation of Israel was divided into two kingdoms after King Solomon died. The Northern kingdom consisting of ten tribes and the Southern kingdom consisting of two Judah and Benjamin Solomon's two sons Jeroboam (Israel) and Rehoboam (Judah) began to reign over the two nations. Later, King Asa reigned for forty one years in Judah. During that same period a total of eight wicked kings ruled in Israel. Eventually Israel was conquered and carried away into captivity by the Assyrians.

Notice II Chronicles 15:9: Then he [King Asa] gathered all Judah and Benjamin, and those who dwelt with them in Ephraim, Manasseh, and Simeon, for they came over to him in great numbers from Israel when they saw that the Lord was with him.

The marginal note for 15:9 says: This indicates that not all people in the ten tribes which constituted the apostate Northern Kingdom of Israel had abandoned God, *many migrated south into Judah.* So I imagine all ten tribes were represented in the mix of Jews in Judah.

We have ungodly people in our culture who don't want any divine standards to which they must be held accountable. But when God leaves a society all hope goes with Him.

So long as you have God – you always have hope! Even
if circumstances collapse, God will keep you!

This problem is very prevalent today in America and other Western countries. Today (4/17/14), CBN News reported that recent research in Great Britain reflects that 60% of Brits have never attended a church service. Too many individuals, families, and communities want to keep God on the outer fringes of their lives. We want Him close enough if we need Him – yet for enough away from us so that He doesn't upset our plans. The more we marginalize God, the worst things get. This is what Paul said in Romans 1:18, *"The wrath of God is revealed from heaven against all ungodliness and unrighteousness of men who suppress the truth in unrighteousness."* Study very carefully verses 19-32 where Paul traced the downward spiral of a culture that excluded God. How do we reverse this downward spiral of our lives? God has a plan that will enable us to function properly if we will just follow His Word. When our lives are in proper relationship with God and each other – He will enable us to live the Christian life as it was meant to be lived.

STUDY GUIDE: CHAPTER 1

1. In a postmodern world the rational arguments for the existence of God are _____ and _____.

2. A goal for the body of Christ is to accept diversity _____ as a restoration reality.

3. The early church born on the Day of Pentecost lasted until _____.

4. "Be holy, because I am holy" is to be understood as standing for the _____ _____.

5. The Catholic Church pointed to the _____ _____; the church that is _____ has all the truth – Jesus Christ.

6. Christians are the _____ of the world and the _____ of the earth.

7. There is no _____ force like the _____ of a common religion.

8. The church is _____ not only in the sense that it is worldwide, but in the sense that it is _____ in the atonement.

9. After dark, Christians were _____ for Nero's garden.

10. In 1973 _____ became legal.

11. List one indicator that God has withdrawn His restraint from a society _____.

12. List three essentials missing from Israel when they forgot God
_____
_____.

13. As long as you always have _____, you will always have _____.

14. It was God who allowed Israel to go into _____ by the _____.

15. King Asa ruled in Judah for _____ years and during this same period in Israel had _____ kings.

CHAPTER 2

COMPROMISE IS A NO-NO!

As part of the secular humanism agenda and their attack against God and the things of God in this nation; they often stress that not all of the founding fathers were Christians. That is without a doubt true, but what is not being discussed or defended is the Christian consensus that was in place at the time. Something is subtly happening in the United States which is causing a gigantic shift in our culture; which is totally anti-Christian and humanistically oriented.

Satan has been working very subtly his destructive plan on the cultural, social, moral, legal, educational and governmental foundations of our nation. Since the beginning of the past century, he has allied with the secularists' and religionists' agenda. His hidden agenda is to destroy America's biblical worldview. Together they have come a long way toward reaching many of their goals over the past thirty years?

What's new?

It is apparent that many people including some professing Christians have absolutely no idea in what areas the battles are really raging in our culture; yet they are violently opposed to God's moral Law and biblical truth at every point including:

- Denial of the existence of God
- Denial of the supernatural
- Belief in the total sufficiency of science and human reason
- Denial of the fall and depravity of humanity

- Denial of the Deity of Christ
- Denial of the finished work of Christ
- Denial of the truths of God's Word
- Destruction of the Bible
- Belief that man is the measure of all things[13]

I headed this section, "What's new?" Within the past thirty to 40 years a new consensus, secular humanism has taken ahold of our national society. The problem we face as a result of this shift is a fundamental change in the way people think, view the world and life as a whole.

A couple of decades ago pastors and teachers as myself were struggling to maintain the Christian consensus through civic and community involvement with people that were at least raised up during the time going to church was fashionable. There was enough "talking about Jesus" in the workplace and community that even sinners believed that God created the heavens and the earth, and hell really exists. Today many Christians are beginning to accept the lie that Christianity is a private matter; that it is politically incorrect to practice it outside the four walls of the church building. Additionally, they are deceiving many to believe that our public witness and involvement in evangelism in the marketplace is illegal. God forbid!

Compromise

In the 70's and 80's the watch word was "containment." The fruits of the 60's were on the vines and the people didn't like what they saw so the best thing to do was hide it away in certain areas of the community and city. Realizing that this "whatever you want to name it" was too big to get a handle on, so let's just contain Christianity and the things of God personal and private. This diabolical seed [thought] conceived and hatched in academia is fast becoming the entire Western World's worldview that believes:

- We live in a universe that is ultimately silent, with no meaning and purpose.
- We have no basis for **law, morality,** and **no value** for human life.
- All is **relative.**

So humanity is left with nothing to fill the void; but **hedonism** and **materialism** aided by **individualism, multiculturalism, intellectualism** and any number of other "isms" that may be lurking in the shadows. This ideology will only lead to damnation for those who embrace it.

We hear much these days about "compromise" in our legislative branch of Government. Though presently practiced very little; it is a political term. However, nothing positive is expressed of it in the Bible. Simply because those of us who are stewards of the Word do not have the authority to modify or compromise what God has deemed truth. So truth is absolute and non-negotiable.

Satan has America locked in a life and death struggle over what happens not only in the heavens, but also in their day to day living. The truths of the Christian faith stand in antithesis to the **thoughts, ideas** and **immorality** of this present world.

Truth must be defended and not compromised in teaching and practical application. Truth demands confrontation! Paul admonishes us to speak the truth in love. Much of the church has not been active in the battle or even able to see that we are in a battle. Seldom do we confront. When it comes to the **issues of the day** much of what the church is adding to the conversation is the same thing the world is saying. God forbid!

Watch your **thoughts**, they become **words**, watch your words, they become **actions**, watch your actions, they become **habits**, watch your habits, they become **character**, watch your character, it become your destiny.

Ralph Waldo Emerson

Emerson's key words form the acronym: **W.A.T.C.H.**

Words
Actions
Thoughts
Character
Habits

*"Set a **watch**, O Lord before my mouth, and keep the door of my lips."*

Another writer substituted the word companions for character:

Companions – birds of a feather flock together. Evil communications corrupt good manners. Be careful what friendships you make. We cannot touch filth and remain undefiled.

There has been compromise on the issues, when we:

- Do not take a clear stand on matters of life and death.
- Deny the power of the Scriptures to confront the spirit of this world.
- Allow the further slide of the culture into degradation.

So we must admit it is the Christian church that is compromising [giving in] to the spirit of the world around us, allowing the wisdom of the world, to remove the church from standing against further meltdown of the culture. The effectiveness of the Scripture in the church and culture is being destroyed by:

- Biblical ignorance
- Theological error from individualistic interpretation
- A weakened view of the Bible,
- No longer affirming or defending all of the truth the Bible teaches
- Compromising on sinful issues,
- Cultural infiltration and influence.

Satan is trying to wear down the saints. Are we as Christians going to draw a line in the sand publicly and stand in the supernatural power of the Holy Spirit and advance with our only offensive weapon, the truths of God's Word?

The Armor of God

The Scriptures make clear that we are locked in a battle of cosmic proportions.

For our struggles is not against flesh and blood, but against the rulers, against the authorities, against the powers of this dark world and against spiritual forces of evil in the heavenly realms (Ephesians 6:12) (AMP).

The Apostle John says, *"The whole world is under the control of the evil one"* (1 John 5:19) (AMP).

It is a life or death struggle for the **minds** and **souls** of human beings for all eternity – but it is also a life or death struggle over human life here on the earth:

- Unborn children are being killed by the thousands here in the United States each year.
- We have no freedom of speech when it comes to speaking of God and the truths of His Word in public schools.
- Every form of sexual perversion is being promoted as normal to include pedophilia, same sex marriages, cohabitation, and illegitimacy.
- Today the biblical model of marriage and family is under attack.
- No-fault divorces have become the norm, but so have multiple re-marriages.
- In many quarters the thinking is, those over sixty five along with the disabled of all ages are expendable when they are no longer physically able to contribute to society? Euthanasia is not unthinkable!

Sadly, very few Christians have truly understood the battle we are in. Few have taken a strong stand against the spirit of this world as it destroys our culture and the Christian biblical worldview that once shaped this country.

Secular humanism and religious Christianity have moved almost at will claiming to be autonomous and crushing all that we cherish and have labored so hard to attain in their paths. We have a responsibility to the next generation. The songwriter stated it so beautifully when he wrote this song of commitment:

A Charge to Keep I Have

1. A charge to keep I have, A God to glorify,
2. To serve the present age, My calling to fulfill;

3. Arm me with watchful care As in thy sight to live,
4. Help me to watch and pray, And still on thee rely,
    A never dying soul to save, And fit it for the sky.
    O may it all my pow'ers engage to do my Master's will!
    And now thy servant, Lord prepare A strict account to give!
    O let me not my trust be-tray, But press to realms on
    high. A-men

– Charles Wesley

If we don't stand [NOW] our children and children's children will have little solid ground on which to stand or hope for being salt and light to their charge. If we stand with the intention of winning we must commit to fighting with the only weapon that will be effective, the Word of God wielded by:

*   A life committed to Christ
*   A life founded on truth
*   A life lived in righteousness
*   A life grounded in the gospel

The Apostle Paul writes,

*"Finally, be strong in the Lord and in His mighty power. Put on the full armor of God so that you can take your stand against the devil's schemes … Therefore put on the full armor of God, so that when the day of evil comes, you may be able to stand your ground, and after you have done everything, to stand. Stand firm then, with your belt of truth buckled around your waist, with the breastplate of righteousness in place, and with your feet fitted with the readiness that comes from the gospel of peace. In addition to all of this, take up the shield of faith, with which you can extinguish all the flaming arrows of the evil one. Take the helmet of salvation and **the sword of the Spirit,** which is the Word of God; and praying in the Spirit on all occasions with all kinds of prayers and requests. With this in mind, be alert and always keep on praying for all the saints."* (Ephesians 6:10, 11, 13-18) [AB].

Notice the weapons listed so for are defensive weapons to defend us against the devil's attacks. The *only offensive weapon* mentioned is "the sword of the Spirit," which is the Word of God." The Bible is the weapon which enables us to enter the battle with our Lord on the offensive in defeating the spiritual hosts of wickedness.

Word of God – by Charles Spurgeon

Why is the Word of God so effective in Spiritual battle? A warrior is careful as to the quality of his sword. If a man had made his own sword, had tempered the metal, had passed the blade through many fires and worked it to perfection, then he would feel confidence in his sword. The Holy Spirit has made this Book Himself: every portion of it bears His initial impress, and thus He has a true Jerusalem blade of heavenly quality. He delights to use a weapon so divinely made, and He does use it gloriously.

The Word of God is the sword of the Spirit because the Spirit puts the edge upon it. It is because the Spirit is in it that the sword is so sharp. I believe in the inspiration of the Holy Scripture, not only in the day it was written but onward, and even to this day. The Holy Spirit still breathes through the chosen words. The sword would have no edge at all if it were not for the Spirit's presence within it and His perpetual working by it. The Holy Spirit rides in the chariot of Scripture and not in the wagon of modern thought. Scripture is that Ark of the Covenant that contains the golden pot of manna and bears above it the divine light of God's shining. The Spirit of God works in, by, through and with the Word, and if we keep that Word, the Holy Spirit will keep with us and make our testimony to be a thing of power.

You must go to the training ground of the Holy Spirit to be made an expert swordsman. The Holy Spirit must take the things of Christ and show them to us. He must teach us how to grip this sword by faith and how to hold it by watchfulness so as to parry the adversary's thrust and carry the war into the foe's territory. He is well taught who can swing this great two-edged sword to and fro, mowing a lane through the midst of his opponents and conquering to the end. It may take a long time to learn this art, but we have a skillful Teacher. I know that I need daily to be taught how to use this mysterious weapon, which is capable of so much more than I have yet supposed. It is the sword of the Spirit, adapted for the use of an Almighty arm and therefore equal to the doing of far more than we think. Holy Spirit, teach us new feats of arms by this Your sword![14]

STUDY GUIDE: CHAPTER 2

1. Part of the secular humanism agenda is their deadly attack against _____ and the _____ _____ in America.

2. The _____ concencus has replaced the _____ _____ in our society.

3. List three negatives in society due to the rise of the secular consensus in our society:
   a.
   b.
   c.

4. In the absence of law and morality due to relativism in the culture only _____ and _____ are left to fill the void.

5. We are in a struggle for our lives as Satan seeks the _____ and _____ of human beings for all eternity.

6. _____and _____ are deadly weapons Satan is using against the _____ _____ worldview.

7. The only offensive weapon the believer has against Satan's darts is the _____ of the _____ .

8. January 22, 2014 marked the 41st anniversary of _____ versus _____ [abortions].

9. Stewards of the Word of God do not have the _____ to modify _____ of what God has deemed truth.

10. Truth must be _____ and not compromised in teaching and _____ application.

11. The biblical concept of _____ and _____ is under heavy fire today.

12. Secular humanism and religious Christianity is striving to crush all that we _____ and _____ so hard for in their path.

13. If we don't make a stand today future _____ will have no foundation on which _____.

14. List four pieces of the armor of God below:
    a.
    b.
    c.
    d.

15. We are admonished to keep praying for _____.

CHAPTER 3

WARM AND MODEL CHRISTIANS

A man's wife often described him as such a warm and model person. One day he decided to check out what she really meant by this wonderful compliment. Grabbing the closest dictionary he looked up the definitions:

- Warm means – not so hot.
- Model means – a small imitation of the real thing.

Many of our citizens are going around hearing and believing the great compliment that America is a Christian nation and people in other lands are awe struck by the American Dream. Yet the least bit of true social research [of the people themselves] reveals that this nation is probably the most Christian nation, when compared to most others. This is true in spite of the one-sided secularly oriented reports from the government, media and education. America remains the center of Christianity, after three hundred years as such.

I believe the spirit of this world, Satan, has an ongoing campaign to deceive the world and discourage God's people by projecting a picture through [media and education] which he controls; that leads many to believe that secular humanism and the other "isms" have triumphed over true Christianity. God forbid! While much media attention is directed toward events happening in Russia, the Middle East, the African Continent and other parts of the world; all of that may be necessary for profits, however, few people realize that perhaps America has indeed become the *major* spiritual war zone affecting the entire world in these last days.

Certainly Satan wants to focus the problem *away from the Bible;* which has been his strategy for more than one hundred years. He has intensified his efforts in these last days because his time is short and he knows it. In the meantime, every day we are hit with every imaginable way to *modify* or *compromise* biblical standards.

As in the illustration above we had better get our hands on a new cultural dictionary; because much of the terminology that marked this nation's morals and values under God have been:

Demolished or

• Redefined in every discipline, area, and manner of life.

Rapid morality breakdown

Many Christian communities were hit with a broadside as reality began to sink in that our lawyers, judges and politicians are inventing new terminology and language of the law to get around **God's moral Law** by misinterpreting **the Constitution of the United States;** both of which have been so crucial for this great nation **"of the people."** Many Christians will quickly admit that they do not understand the *root cause* of such a rapid breakdown in our societal moral fiber or how the enemy was able to launch and conduct such a subtle and successful spiritual warfare campaign against us.

The Root Cause

In his book, *the Foundations of Christian Doctrine,* Dr. Kevin J. Conner informs us that based on the Law of Double Reference (for example: *speaking of or to one person there is reference to another person beyond and behind them* (Study Genesis 3:14-15; Matthew 16:23). Daniel's prophecy **confirms** the fact that there are princes of Satan's kingdom behind the princes of the **world** kingdoms. (Study Daniel 8:20-21; 10:10-13, 20-21)

Ezekiel 28:1-19 and Isaiah 14:4-23 should be studied carefully concerning Satan's origin and fall. Satan is a real personality. He is evil personified and characteristics and activities are ascribed to him:[15]

- Satan is not an impersonal influence or power.
- He is the originator of rebellion against divine authority (1 John 3:8; Ephesians 2:2).
- Personal pronouns, intelligence, knowledge, will and action are attributed to him (Study Job 1:8; 2:1-2; Zechariah 3:1; II Corinthians 2:11; Matthew 4:6; Revelation 12:12; II Timothy 2:26; Matthew 25:41; Isaiah 14:12-13).
- He is a created being, therefore dependent upon God for his very existence (see Ezekiel 28:13, 15).
- He was once in truth (see John 8:44).
- He is the master of deception (Study Genesis 3:1-4; II Corinthians 11:3; 1Timothy 2:14; II Corinthians 11:13-15; John 8:44; II Thessalonians 2:9-10).
- He seeks to afflict physically and mentally (see I Corinthians 5:5; Luke 13:16; II Corinthians 12:7).[16]
- Satan and his hosts are involved in a great spiritual war against God and His Kingdom (Study carefully I Chronicles 21:1; Acts 10:38; Revelation 2:10; 12:13, 17; 13:7; I Thessalonians 2:18; I Peter 5:8; Revelation 12:4; II Timothy 2:25-26).
- Death is the greatest power of Satan manifested, but Jesus has conquered death by His resurrection (see Hebrews 2:14; Jude 9; 1 John 3:12; John 8:44).

Never in the history of humankind have Christians been subject to such heavy temptations as those of our mass communication systems [internet, social media etc.] with which to mix and become *contaminated* by the prince of this world's systems. A few months ago I heard on the news that a young teenager caused four deaths in a fatal accident while driving under the influence of alcohol. According to the media his defense lawyer coined a new word and got the teen off with counseling and rehab. The term he used was "affluenza." Supposedly to mean, his family's riches had given him such a superiority complex that the right-a-way belonged to him. Sad! This type of corruption is repeated daily in courtrooms and judges' chambers across this nation. In a recent newscast it was reported that the parents have paid only one third of the counseling/ rehabilitation costs.

The world is the world! However, many churches may not call what they are doing "affluenza," but it amounts to the same type accommodation and compromise. It has not dawned on many yet just how far the establishment of "no absolutes" has taken control of our society. Where there was once a standard of ethics for all, now each entity establishes its own ethics. In every field these ethics are mostly driven by monetary profits at every level. Because much of the church has been bitten by this bug – many have lost their effectiviness as Christ's deterrent facing darkness and evil. A visit to these churches in many cases leaves a bad taste.

Satan's worldly contamination has taken its toll on our identity as the body of Christ fulfilling its mission as salt and light, "Christ's representatives in the world." The so-called "new morality" developed over the past thirty or forty years has definitely influenced the Christian community much more than the Christian community has influenced the world from whence it came. We have become more tolerant and *indifferent* toward many of the sins in the world. Today people feel free to openly display and promote their sins, not only by their lifestyles but also through the media that is available to everyone. They want no God! Everybody is coming out now, it seems fashionable these days to announce publicly that I am an atheist, a gay or we are cohabitating with so and so. The spirit of the world is flaunting the secular attitude that, "this is all there is – so be happy, have fun and get all you can for when it's all over and you die; and that's all folks!" Wrong! It's just the beginning. We will leave time when we die and enter eternity. How we enter eternity is how we will spend it. If you leave this life without Christ in your heart and life then expect eternity without Him. Ignorance of "truth" will not be excused on the coming day of reckoning. Listen to a pagan king's expression of the God of heaven after defying Him, *"I Nebuchadnezzar, praise and honor the King of heaven, all of whose works are truth, and His ways justice. And those who walk in pride He is able to put down"*(Daniel 4:37).

"The wicked shall be turned into hell, and all nations that forget God"
(Psalm 9:17).

Rights come from our Creator not the Government

Does power flow FROM the God of heaven TO the rulers then TO the people, as ancient, medieval and post Renaissance monarchs claimed, or does power flow FROM the God of heaven TO the people then TO the rulers, as America's founders claimed?

Thomas Jefferson explained in the Declaration, that power flowed from the Creator to the people, and the government derived its power *"from the consent of the governed."*[17]

President Eisenhower told the American Legion's Back to God Program, February 20, 1955:

The Founding Fathers .... recognizing God as the author of individual rights, declared that the purpose of government is to secure those rights. In many lands the State claims to be the author of human rights ..... if the State gives rights, it can .... and *inevitably* take away those rights.

Dwight D. Eisenhower wrote in an article published in the *Episcopal Church news Magazine:*

The founding fathers had to refer to the Creator in order to make their revolutionary experiment make sense; it was because "all men are endowed by the Creator with certain inalienable rights" that men could dare to be free.[18]

No God the State becomes god

President John F. Kennedy stated in his *Inaugural Address,* 1961:

The rights of man come not from the generosity of the state, but from the hand of God.

But **if** there is no GOD, where do rights come from, except the generosity of the STATE."[19]

Without a God as the source for citizens' rights, the State becomes the source of rights. The State, then, becomes the *new god,* and what the State "giveth," the State can "taketh awayeth!"

Clarence E. Manion, Professor of Constitutional Law and Dean of the Notre Dame College of Law, as quoted in Verne Paul Kaub's book, *Collectivism Challenges Christianity* (1946), stated:

"Look closely at these self-evident truths, these imperishable articles of American Faith upon which our government is firmly based:

- **First** and foremost is the existence of **God.**
- **Then** the **truth** came that all men are equal in the sight of God.
- **Third** is the fact of God's great gift of **inalienable rights** to every person on earth.
- **Then** follows the true and single purpose for all American Government, namely, to preserve and protect these God-made rights of God-made man.[20]

In his book, *Change to Chains,* William J. Federer states, the Constitution was written to separate power into executive, legislature, and judicial branches, **but** since then other "branches" of power have emerged, such as unions, judges, trial lawyers, lobbyists, environmental groups, financial institutions, and perhaps the most significant, education and media. In America:

The COUNTRY is controlled by LAWS
LAWS are controlled by POLITICIANS
POLITICIANS are controlled by VOTERS
VOTERS are controlled by PUBLIC OPINION
PUBLIC OPINION is controlled by the MEDIA (News,
Hollywood, Internet etc.) and EDUCATION
So **whoever** controls MEDIA and
EDUCATION – controls the
COUNTRY

This identification and influencing of power is basic to human nature, as in a traditional home a child knows that father has the final say, but he complains to mother to persuade father; or he bothers his big sister to complain to mother to persuade father, or he bribes brother to bother big sister to complain to mother to persuade father!

If a child can figure out where the power sits and how to get his or her way, it is not that difficult for some to figure out that in **America** the power sits with the **laws,** but to change them one must influence **politicians** by influencing **voters** by influencing **public opinion** by controlling **media and education!** Politicians **FEAR** public opinion, therefore those desiring to affect the direction of the country must utilize education, media and the Internet.[21]

An illustration from the Gospel of Matthew tells of rulers being kept in check because they feared a negative public opinion spreading among the people (see chapter 21:23-27 KJV):

> *And when he was come into the temple,*
> *the chief priests and the elders of the people*
> *came unto him as he was teaching, and said, "By*
> *what authority doest thou these things, and*
> *who gave thee this authority?"*
> *And Jesus answered and said unto them,*
> *"I also will ask you one thing, which if ye tell*
> *me, I like wise will tell you by what authority*
> *I do these things. The baptism of John, whence*
> *was it? From heaven or of men?"*
> *And they reasoned with themselves,*
> *saying, "If we shall say, From heaven; he will*
> *say unto us, Why did ye not then believe him?"*
> *But if we shall say, Of men; WE FEAR THE*
> *PEOPLE; for all hold John as a prophet."*
> *And they answered Jesus, and said, "We cannot tell."*
> *And he said unto them, "Neither tell I you*
> *By what authority I do these things."*

The Gospel of Mark tells of a political ruler swayed because he was afraid of the negative public opinion spreading among the people, (see chapter 15:9-15 KJV):

> *But Pilate answered them saying, will ye that*
> *I release unto you the King of the Jews?" For he knew*
> *that the chief priests had delivered him for envy.*
> *BUT THE CHIEF PRIESTS MOVED THE PEOPLE,*

> *that he should rather release Barabbas unto them.*
> *And Pilate answered and said again unto them,*
> *"What will ye then that I shall do unto him*
> *whom ye call the King of the Jews?"*
> *And they cried out again, "Crucify him."*
> *Then Pilate said unto them,*
> *"Crucify him."*
> *And so Pilate, WILLING TO CONTENT THE PEOPLE,*
> *released Barabbas unto them, and delivered*
> *Jesus, when he had scourged him, to be crucified.*

A parable of persistence affecting political leaders is in the Gospel of Luke, (Chapter 18:1-5) KJV:

> *He spake a parable unto them to this end,*
> *that men ought always to pray, and not to faint;*
> *saying, "There was in a city, a judge, which feared*
> *not God, neither regarded man: And there was*
> *a widow in that city; and she came unto him, saying,*
> *'Avenge me of mine adversary.'*
> *And he would not for a while: but afterward*
> *he said within himself, "Though I fear not God,*
> *nor regard man; YET BECAUSE THIS WIDOW*
> *TROUBLETH ME, I will avenge her,*
> *LEST BY HER CONTINUAL COMING*
> *SHE WEARY ME."*

What will the world be like before the Lord returns? People will go about the world daily, not fearing God, marrying and eating and drinking, and having fun then; Christ will come and they will not be prepared to meet Him. In Noah's day, there was a great deal of **violence** (see Genesis 6:11, 13); and in Lot's time, men gave themselves over to **unnatural lusts** (see Genesis 19:4-11; Romans 1:21). Both of these characteristics are fast becoming the norm in our day. In the days of our preceding Scripture, it was difficult for poor widows to get justice because they had no means for bribing the officers who would get the judge to act. However, this widow would not quit until the judge granted what was due her.

If a selfish non God-fearing judge finally meets the needs of the poor widow, how much more will the Heavenly Father meet the needs of His own children when they cry to Him? Please note, this parable is not urging us to "pester God" until He finally acts; it is saying that we do not need to pester Him because He is ready to answer His children's prayers.

- The widow had no lawyer – but we have a High Priest in heaven.
- She had no promises – but we have a Bible full of promises for us to claim.
- She was an outsider – but we are the children of God.

Oh! What a blessing it is to have the privilege to pray!

The will of a minority

In the period prior to past judgments our graceful Father has warned us through faithful men and on occasion angels from heaven. The world today is like that of Noah and Lot's day "business as usual" with little concern or fear for the warnings God sends.

Is the will of the people still reflected in government? The "will of the people" is no longer the law of the land in the area of religious beliefs. Poll after poll showed that 80.2 percent of the population in United States held Judeo-Christian beliefs in 2007 reported the CIA.gov website's World Facebook (2007). Backroom arm twisting, pork barrel bribes and disinformation campaigns have resulted in many bills being passed by Congress and signed by the sitting president for which the people expressed their displeasure – many time on moral grounds. In his farewell address September 19, 1796, George Washington, the very first president of the United States warned:

And a fatal tendency ...... to put, in the place of the delegated will of the Nation, **the will of a party – often a small but artful and enterprising minority** ..... Cunning, ambitious, and unprincipled men will be enabled to subvert the power of the people and to usurp for themselves the reins of government. The *American Religious Identification Survey* (2001), conducted by the Graduate Center, City University of New York, reported:

77.8 percent of the U.S. population held Judeo-Christian beliefs (52 percent Protestant, 24.5 Catholic, 1.3 percent Jewish). The rest of the population was:

0.5 percent Muslim

0.5 percent Buddhist

0.5 percent Agnostic

0.4 percent Hindu

0.3 percent Unitarian-Universalists

0.1 percent Wiccan-Pagan-Druid

13.2 percent Secular

6.3 percent Spiritualist-Native American-Baha'i-New Age Scientology-Humanist-Deist-Taoist-Eckankar, and

Only 0.4 percent atheist

Yet, it is apparent that these groups are successfully working with **judges** to discriminate against traditional Judeo-Christian beliefs in favor of secular humanism, atheism, and sometimes Islam.[22] If the will of the majority of **"the people"** is not reflected in the laws, then the country is no longer **"democratic."** [**No longer a Democracy**]!

The Separation of Church and State?

The Community of Faith has heard much falsely interpreted information from the Supreme Court and some national and state leaders concerning the separation of church and state. The *misinterpretation* concerns what Thomas Jefferson wrote about the *wall of separation* between church and state. I quote:

> *"I contemplate with sovereign reverence that act of the whole American people which declared that their legislature should make no law respecting an establishment of religion, or prohibiting the free exercise thereof; thus building a wall of separation between Church & State."*

The limitation in the First Amendment is upon Congress, **not** the churches. Jefferson's metaphor was a wall that prevented the federal government from intruding on religion in the states or denying the people the right of free exercise of religion.

In their book, Personal Faith-Public Policy, Harry Jackson and Tony Perkins explains, At the time the First Amendment was written and ratified, a number of the fifteen states had established state churches. The First Amendment did not change that. The founders were concerned that the federal government would try to take over the churches and use them for its own purposes.[23]

Further, they did not fear that Christians would influence the government. Christians were the government. Churches, members of the clergy, and parishioners have been, and remain, free in this country to participate in public policy debates on any subject. I personally remember back in the fifties and sixties, with my father who was a pastor, it was a common practice for pastors to preach prior to an election telling members which candidates were worthy of their support. During the early part of my own pastoral experience this continued to be the practice in many communities of faith. However, I assure you the reason was to avoid corrupted candidates and morality, not for monetary gain nor political. This was necessary [to explain the politicians' platforms] due to wide-spread illiteracy in society at that time. During the past ten years, intolerance toward Christians and Christianity has increased at an alarming rate. An anti-Christian activism position is subtly spreading here in the United States. It is beginning to show its head (Satan) in the churches.

It seems that many on church rolls would rather be religious and lost; than to be obedient to the Lordship of Christ and have eternal life. Have we returned to Babel?
– Jay R. Leach

The failure of the church to participate in the shaping of public policy has resulted in limitation of our ability to openly evangelize the lost. We must encourage the bold standing of *all* the people of God in defense of the Cross of Christ and the truths it proclaims that all humanity might be set free!

STUDY GUIDE: CHAPTER 3

1. America has been the center of Christianity in the West for the past _____ years.

2. Most Christians do not understand the _____ _____ of the rapid breakdown in our societal moral fiber.

3. Write out Psalm 9:17 and explain where you think America stands on a scale of 1 ------------ 10.

4. List at least three powers that are challenging the three branches of the government's decisions today:

5. What was the political ruler's greatest fear in the Mark:9-15?

6. Traditional Judeo-Christian beliefs are threatened by groups working with _____ .

7. What happens when the _____ of the people is not _____ in the _____, then the country is no longer _____ .

8. Every America citizen has _____ rights.

9. Many groups are successfully working with judges to discriminate against traditional _____ beliefs in favor of _____ _____, _____ and sometimes _____.

10. If the will of the majority of "_____ _____" is not reflected in the laws, then the country is no longer _____.

11. Politicians are influenced by _____ _____.

12. Whoever controls media and education controls _____.

13. Death was _____ greatest _____ but Jesus has conquered _____.

14. However we enter _____ is how we will spend it.

15. The founding fathers recognized God as the _____ of _____ rights.

SECTION II
I CAN KNOW THE WAY

CHAPTER 4

THE NARROW WAY

The Bible teaches that Satan has always used two distinct methods in his attacks on the people of God, persecution and deception. Each has the same goal: to keep God's people from fulfilling their mission as the salt of the earth and the light [as Christ's representatives] in this world of darkness. Persecution is easy to detect, but deception is much more difficult.

Persecution

Persecution – is an attack against the body that causes physical harm. The idea is to get us to **deny** our relationship with Christ **to avoid persecution.** At the same time, persecution always separates the true believers from those who merely profess the faith. This is seen even today as humanists and religionists apply the slightest bit of pressure the professors begin to fall away and abandon their allegiance to Christ and His church. Speak out against immorality, and you're hated. Stand up for traditional marriage, and the traditional family and you will be classified an antiquated bigot or worse. Those of us who claim that Jesus is the only way to God are considered narrow minded fanatics. In fact that very accusation prompted this book. As we continue to preach and teach the true truth of God's Word, we will find ourselves with more acquaintances and fewer true ministry friends. From now until the rapture, I believe things will grow worse as Christians and Christianity are pushed further toward marginalization in society. Daily our biblical worldview and values are becoming increasingly unpopular and despised by many. If the church does not remain vigilant the day might come through some atheistic lawmaker or judge trying to make the claim that it is politically incorrect to preach and teach the truths of the Bible.

Jesus warned us that we would be hated. We are to counter hatred with love; never should we lose our loyalty to our Lord and Savior, Jesus Christ. It's hard to imagine some of the things prophesied to take place during the Tribulation, but those persons who are truly studying God's Word should see that in the societal atmosphere there is a building turbulence that may erupt before the rapture.

Because it is not of media interest yet, it has not been made public; however people lose jobs and suffer other ills because of their love and obedience to Christ. True colors will show when we have to give up family members that they may be arrested. Being told what not to preach and teach; and banned from street evangelism. Failure to comply may result in monetary fines, loss of government benefits, or even death!

It is also difficult to believe how much the world *already* dislikes God, Christians and the things of God. Another phenomenon is the number of false teachers already on the scene misleading multitudes, including many who formerly professed faith in Christ. Biblical morals and values will increasingly disappear as we witness the increase of wickedness and lawlessness as was prophesied (see Mathew 24:12).

Through persecution we notice:

- Some 70 million faithful Christians have been killed over the last 2000 years. 45.5 million or 65% were killed in the 20th century.
- Some 45,400,000 Christians were killed between 1900 and 2000.
- Since 1950, 13,300,000 Christians have been killed.
- The average number of Christians killed annually is 160,000.
- Among the annual number killed from major world religions killed annually: 80 million (Islam), 70 million (Christian), 20 million (Hindu), 10 million (Buddhism), and 9 million (Judaism).[24]

Persecution of the church worldwide continues to increase at an alarming rate. America has enjoyed freedom from religious persecution over the centuries; and remains the world center for Christian witness. The Scriptures teach us what history confirms, it is easy to see why the devil has launched an all-out spiritual attack [of deception] against our country.

Satan is doing everything he can to **change every law or standard** in this country that is based on God's moral law and Christian standards!

Peter admonishes us,

"Be sober, be vigilant, because your adversary the devil walks about like a roaring lion, seeking whom he may devour. Resist him, steadfast in the faith" (1 Peter 5:8, 9a).

Satan is both cunning and cruel. He attacks when least expected and desires to destroy completely those whom he attacks. The body of Christ in America must understand what is taking place.

Certainly prophetic Scriptures **warn us** that this will happen in the last days as Satan sees that his time is running out. I pray that through this brief review of persecution, you will see just how wicked, cruel and ruthless our enemy, Satan really is.

The Apostle Peter counsels the Church to be:

- Sober – to be self-disciplined, to think spiritually and not foolishly.
- Vigilant – to remain alert to the spiritual pitfalls of life and take appropriate steps to make certain that we do not stumble.
- Resist – to fight rather than to run. Victory comes when we remain committed to God, because **He is greater than our enemy!** Praise God!

Consider the lives of the Apostles, who were all martyred for the "faith" except the Apostle John:

- Listen to one who recently experienced persecution, when asked why God would allow him to suffer such persecution commented:
  "Not only would He not kill our enemies for us, but He would empower us to love them while they killed us."

- Another missionary killed in 1956 by headhunters in Ecuador stated,

---

"He is no fool who gives what he cannot keep to gain what he cannot lose."
Jim Ellliot, Missionary 1956[25]

Deception

While Satan uses persecution and deception; deception has been his primary method of attacking Christians and the church in America. Israel experienced persecution and deception for most of its history.

Pride makes us susceptible to deception. Humility is your protection from deception.

Deception – is a demonic attack through our mind tempting our sinful nature; and using the lust of the eye, the lust of the flesh, and the pride of life to disobey God's Word:

- By getting some Christians to accept deceptive philosophies that are contrary to the truths of God's Word.
- By making wrong things appear to be innocent.
- By performing their acts of seduction in lewd manners attempting to make their enticements irresistible.
- By trying to make the difference between black and white a shade of gray, thus attempting to create by illusion an area that is really non-existent.

If you don't know the Word of God, diligently seek righteousness, and hate every evil way, you will easily become susceptible to deceiving spirits. **This is no longer a prophetic future danger in this country, but a present reality in the last days.** The Scripture is absolutely clear that deception will be a primary method in which Satan will attack Christians in the last days. The Apostle Paul writes,

*"Now the Spirit expressly says that in latter times some will depart from the faith, giving heed to **deceiving spirits** and **doctrines of demons** speaking lies in hypocrisy, having their own consciences seared with a hot iron"* (1 Timothy 4:1, 2).

This is reality today as:

Some people are departing from the truths of God's Word (see Daniel 7:25; 8:23; Matthew 24:4-12).

- Some are standing away from "their faith" (see 1 Timothy 1:19-20).
- Some are failing to walk obediently (see John 19:25-27; 1 Corinthians 3:1-3; 11:29-30).

It must be emphasized in our churches that continued growth and sanctification occurs through *the truths of God's Word* and *instructions in sound doctrine.*

Discipline in godliness affects both the present and future aspects of the Christian's life. The present aspect includes **obedience** and a life of **purpose** (see John 10:10). The future aspect involves greater **rewards** in the coming reign of Christ (see 1 Corinthians 3:10-15; 2 Corinthians 5:9, 20). By its very nature, deception often goes undetected. The only way you can truly detect the use of deception is by examining the fruit produced.

Deception is revealed by its fruit

Satan has been successful in the use of his most prominent weapon, deception. He is as ruthless, wicked and crafty as he was in the beginning when he brought down Eve, then Adam as well as many other Old Testament leaders like Samson, King Saul, King David, King Solomon and many others in the New Testament even unto this present day.

As satanic deception is destroying the Christian moral
standards of the American people – so goes the nation!

The contemporary Scene

The interpretive perspective of the many historical studies of the Fall of
the Roman Empire gives insight that proves the importance and relevancy
of Christianity and the Christian Church to the contemporary scene in
America and the Western Civilization. Of course the selection is related to the
monumental work of Edward Gibbon, originally published in 1787, entitled:
The Decline and Fall of the Roman Empire, Arnold Toynbee's evaluation of the
civilizations that emerged in the past entitled: *A Study of History* and A book
by Adrian Goldsworty entitled: *How Rome Fell: Death of a Superpower.*

Gibbon's General Observations of the Fall

His conclusions as to the causes for the downfall of the Roman
Empire have been summarized as follows:

1. The rapid increase of divorce; and the decrease in understanding
   of the dignity and sanctity of the home, which is the basis of
   human society.
2. Higher and higher taxes and the spending of public monies for
   free bread and circuses for the populace.
3. The mad craze for pleasure; sports becoming every year more
   exciting and more brutal.
4. The building of gigantic armaments when the real enemy was
   within, the decadence of the people.
5. The decay of religion – faith fading into mere form, losing touch
   with life and becoming impotent to warn and guide the people.[26]

Arnold Toynbee's Evaluation of the Fall

Arnold Toynbee made a comprehensive evaluation of 21 past
civilizations entitled: *A Study of History.*[27] Those that failed went through
a cycle that he summarized as follows:

1. Slavery
2. Faith in the Divine
3. Courage
4. Emancipation and independence
5. Prosperity
6. Selfishness
7. Apathy
8. Dependence on welfare state
9. Slavery

In his book, *How Rome Fell: Death of a Superpower*[28] Adrian Goldsworthy compiled a list of reasons for the fall of Rome in the 5th century. He acknowledges that there is no generally accepted explanation for the fall:

1. Adopted foreign gods
2. Accepted slavery
3. Killed people and animals for entertainment
4. Invading tribes with the intention of taking over
5. Personal success overrode the Empire's goals
6. Large government (forgot what they were there for)
7. Political leaders did not set the example by placing the wider good before personal or party interests.
8. Internal problems
9. Use of mercenary armies (loss of command and control)
10. Homosexuality

A comparison of the conditions that prevail in our American society and those that brought the collapse of the Roman Empire will make every conscientious Christian realize the gravity of today's moral problems. An urgent return to the Great Commission that brings the unsaved to a personal knowledge of the transforming power of our Lord and Savior, Jesus Christ is the true answer (see Matthew 28:18-19).

Vast numbers must be reconciled to God through Christ if moral bankruptcy and national disaster is to be avoided. Witnessing Christians must become a part of the solution by dedicating themselves afresh to the expansion of the kingdom of God. Every true Christian can't help but witness to others especially the unsaved. If you had the cure for cancer in your possession, what would you do with it?

Christian leaders at all levels should repent and get back to the Lord's work. Many members of the community of faith have been caught up in sin through satanic deception due to a lack of knowledge of the finished work of Christ. Sexual sin and marriage breakups are at epidemic levels among Christians as well as the surrounding society. Research shows that addictions to pornography have reached critical mass among Christian men and women alike. Our moral condition reads like Sodom and Gomorrah and that of Rome.

Through deception, the lack of a proper biblical world view, and knowledge of the truth, our society flaunts its lusts of the flesh claiming them to be uncontrollable rights; because in the vernacular of secular humanism, this is natural behavior anyway, "What do you expect from animals?"

> *"Now the works of the flesh are evident,*
> *which are:*
> *adultery, fornication, uncleanness,*
> *lewdness, idolatry, sorcery,*
> *hatred, contentions, jealousies,*
> *outbursts of wrath,*
> *selfish ambitions, discussions,*
> *heresies, envy, murders,*
> *drunkenness, revelries,*
> *and the like; of which I tell you beforehand,*
> *just as I also told you in the past,*
> ***that those who practice such things***
> ***will not***
> ***inherit the kingdom of God"***
> (Galatians 5:19-21).

The flesh energized by the demonic in the life of the Christian possesses tremendous potential for the devastation of countless lives. Left to the secular humanistic worldview [no God] the flesh will:

- Direct our choices.
- Make us do what we know we should not do.

This inner conflict between the flesh and the Spirit is a living reality. The only consistent way to overcome the sinful temptations of the flesh is to walk in the power of the Holy Spirit and the truths of God's Word. They work in tandem sanctifying the Christian through his or her spirit. Under the Spirit's guidance and control the Christian is assured of absolute victory over the sinful desires of the flesh. When the lusts of the flesh are free to operate in the Christian's life such behavior is positive proof that the person is not living in the power of the Holy Spirit (see vv. 16, 18, 22, 23) but the "fruit" manifested proves the individual is being energized by Satan and his hosts (see Matthew 16:23; Acts 5:3).

The Manifestation of the true "Fruit of the Spirit"

Despite avid support from the media, education, government and the culture, fruit manifested by the lust of the flesh can in no way diminish the "true fruit" manifested in the mature saints of God. Christians are spiritually *"crucified with Christ"* (Galatians 2:20). We no longer **have to** follow the values and desires of the world (Galatians 6:14). However, it is impossible to apply this spiritual reality to the lusts of the flesh in your own natural power. In v. 16, the Apostle Paul exhorts the Christian to *"walk in the Spirit"* [which means following the Spirit's lead] and he or she will not fulfill the lust of the flesh. He specifically informs us that the production of this fruit is done by the Holy Spirit Himself in the Christian's life. In Romans 8:29, the Apostle Paul states that God desires that the individual character of His own chosen children undergo a conformational process and become like His Son:

"For whom He foreknew,
He also predestined
to be conformed
*to the **image***
of His Son,
that He might
be the firstborn
among many brethren."

Jesus' teaching on the vine, branches and a fruitful harvest serves as an appropriate analogy depicting this process. The accomplished end is one who has developed the same **fruit** that were easily recognizable in His life. Jesus said,

"I am the true vine, and My Father is the vinedresser. Every branch in Me that does not bear fruit He takes away; and every branch that bears fruit He prunes, that it may bear more fruit." (John 15:1-2)

Every branch is said to be *in Christ*. The Apostle Paul uses the phrase "in Christ" to speak of a Christian's legal and family position as a result of God's grace. The emphasis of in Me in the passage, *is our deep, abiding fellowship*. Jesus' purpose was to move His disciples from servants to friends (see vv. 13-15).

This would involve a process of discipline in regard to His commandments. No plant produces *fruit* instantly; fruit is the result of a process. That is also the case with believers. Pruning coincide with "cleanses." Once the fruit appears on the vine, the vinedresser cleanses the fruit of bugs and disease. The spiritual comparison *is cleansing which is accomplished through the Word* (v. 3).

For the branch to produce *more fruit,* **it must abide,** which means to dwell, stay, and settle or to sink in deeper. The way to abide in Christ is to obey Him (Study 15:16; 1 John 3:24). Jesus said, "….. Without Me you can do nothing." (v. 5b)

The believer who lovingly obeys the Word of God produces *much* fruit.

God's Plan for the Christian Life

Contrary to the thinking in many churches today concerning false prophets, Jesus told His disciples, "You will know them by their fruit. What Jesus said about the false prophets also holds true for the true saints of God. You will know them by their fruit! The world watches the lives of professed Christians – therefore they must be able to recognize the true sons of God. *They recognize them by their fruit!*

Jesus did not say, "You will know them by *their miracles."* Nor did He say, "You will know them by *the size of their membership or church building."* He did not even say, *"You will know them by their spiritual gifts."* He said, **"You will know them by their fruits."** In essence, "You will recognize My disciples by their Christ-like character." This is God's development plan for **all of** His children, we are to:

"Enter by the <u>narrow gate;</u> for wide is the gate and broad is the way that leads to destruction, and there are many who go in by it. Because <u>narrow is the gate</u> and DIFFICULT IS THE WAY which leads to life, and there are few who find it" (Matthew 7:13-14).

I stated in an earlier section, Christ *continually* emphasized the difficulty of following Him (Study carefully: Matthew 10:38; 16:24, 25; John 15:18, 19; 16:1-3; Acts 14:22). Salvation is by **grace alone**, but it is not easy, again it calls for:

- Knowledge of the truth
- Repentance
- Submission to Christ as Lord
- A willingness to obey His will, His word and His way

The fruit of the Spirit consists of nine godly character building Christ-like attitudes that characterize the lives of **only** those who belong to God by grace through faith in Jesus Christ. The fruits formed and cultivated in us by the indwelling Holy Spirit are listed in Galatians 5:22, 23:

1. **Love** – The Greek term is "agape" meaning the love of choice, referring not to emotional affection, physical attraction, or a familial bond, but to respect, devotion, and affection that leads to willing, self-sacrificial service (see John 15:13; Romans 5:8; John 3:16-17).

2. **Joy** – is happiness based on unchanging divine promises and kingdom realities. It is the sense of well-being experienced by one who knows all is well in his or her relationship with God. That is joy, in spite of favorable or non-favorable life circumstances (see John 16:20-22).

3. **Peace** – is the inner calm that results from confidence in one's saving relationship with Christ. Like joy, peace is not related to one's circumstances of life (see John 14:37; Romans 8:28; Philippians 4:6-7, 9).

4. **Longsuffering** – refers to the ability to endure injuries inflicted by others and the willingness to accept irritating or painful people and situations (see Ephesians 4:2; Colossians 3:12; 1 Timothy 1:15-16).

5. **Kindness** – is tender concern for others, reflected in a desire to treat others gently, just as the Lord treats all true Christians (see Matthew 11:28-29; 19:13-14; 2 Timothy 2:24).

6. **Goodness** – is moral and spiritual excellence manifested in active kindness (see Romans 5:7; 6:10; 2 Thessalonians 1:11).

7. **Faithfulness** – is loyalty and trustworthiness (see Lamentations 3:22; Philippians 2:7-9; 1 Thessalonians 5:24; Revelation 2:10).

8. **Gentleness** – also translated "meekness" is a humble and gentle attitude that is patiently submissive in every offense, while having no desire for revenge or retribution.

9. **Self-control** – is the restraining of passions and appetites (see 1 Corinthians 9:25; 2 Peter 1:5-6).

It is important to note, these are the *fruit* of the Spirit, not the *gifts* of the Spirit. There is a difference between the two. We find the gifts of the Spirit listed in Romans 12:6-8; 1 Corinthians 12:8-10. These gifts are spiritual graces manifested through the saints by the Spirit accordingly as He wills. A few of these are wisdom, knowledge, prophecy, tongues, interpretation of tongues, helps, faith, and miracles. These graces are imparted to individual saints for the work of ministry.

The means of acquiring the fruit of the Spirit, however, are very different. Fruit *must be cultivated,* requiring much *time* and *effort.* A high cost is required in the development of the fruit of the Spirit. This is the reason many Christians operate in the gifts – **but** don't give evidence of the fruit. *They are simply not willing to pay the price [required of the narrow way].*

Because a Christian is operating in the gifts of the Spirit is no guarantee that he or she possesses the character of Christ – the fruit of the Spirit!

Many believers operating in the Spiritual gifts under great anointing are some of the rudest and unlikable people you can meet. I believe that we have over glamourized the gifts at the expense of the fruit! Again, the reason why so many pursue the gifts and works over the fruit is probably the difficulty of having to cultivate and spend a tremendous amount of time and effort for the harvest. It is those saints who faithfully and obediently "abide in the vine" developing *all* of the fruit who will be manifest.

Christians cannot become selective so that they cultivate and develop only those fruit that offer the least resistance to their flesh. For example: A believer tries to cultivate faith; but not cultivate love and longsuffering. Christians must develop all of the fruit – for no part or section of it is optional!

Christ is coming back for a church conformed to His image. This means that all Christians must be striving to develop one hundred percent of the fruit. Each part of the fruit enables the individual to better cope with adverse situations that arise in this evil day.

Realizing the key place of the fruit of the Spirit in God's plan for our lives; it is imperative that as believers we become knowledgeable about how to cultivate all of the fruit individually and then begin developing the fruit in our lives.

A Christian cannot be a totally successful overcomer if any one part of the fruit is missing in his or her life. That particular area will be the very one the devil will focus his attack!

Though a lot of time and effort is required, remember the rewards are eternal. Though it may seem impossible to cultivate Christ-likeness – our Father expects each of us to succeed through obedience to His Word, our life sustainer. The Word of God clearly explains how to develop each element or part of the whole fruit.

The Spirit of God works tirelessly to manifest this fruit in our lives. When thinking in terms of spiritual growth, we must realize the truth of 1 Corinthians 3:5, 6: *"that it is always God who gives the increase."* The sooner we choose to get started – the sooner our full harvest will manifest!

How would the fruit of the Spirit manifest itself in reality?

Imagine you are a company personnel manager about to hire an employee. A middle-aged man named George applies for the position. He was very impressive in the interview however; you want to check what others who know him might say about him. You send out a request for a reference to his former boss, who reveals the following: "George has great patience with people; situations that frustrate most people do not seem to rattle him. I have known George for the past several years and have had the privilege of observing him in professional, family and religious settings. He always exhibits a strong degree of self-sacrificing love. He is always upbeat, happy and usually displays a great deal of peace. He gets along very well with others. He is kind and actively caring toward those around him. George has integrity and deeply held convictions that produce a great work ethic. His faith certainly causes him to move the ball downfield when our team needs to score. Although he is a gentleman and meek in nature, he also exercises great self-control."[29]

If you received such a reference, would you hire George? I would. We should cultivate the same reputation! When we look at George, we see Christ-likeness or the fruit of the Spirit personified in the marketplace. What would he probably face in today's job market? Why?

STUDY GUIDE: CHAPTER 4

1. What is the positive proof that a Christian is not living in the power of the Holy Spirit? Explain below:

2. The Bible teaches that Satan uses two distinct methods of attack: _____ and _____ against believers.

3. The number of Christians killed annually around the world through persecution is approximately _____ .

4. The Apostle Peter admonishes the believers to be _____ and to _____ .

5. Satan tempts believers using the lust of the eyes, the lusts of the flesh, and the pride of life to _____ _____ .

6. Some people are departing from the truths of _____ _____ .

7. The _____ standards in America are being destroyed through _____ .

8. A secular worldview in the flesh will _____ your choices and do _____ we should not.

9. As crucified Christians, we no longer have to follow the _____ and _____ of the world.

10. God desires that the individual _____ of His choosing be _____ to the _____ of His Son.

11. How are true sons of God recognized _____?

12. Why are people drawn to the gifts of the Spirit over the fruit of the Spirit? Explain below:

13. List five parts of the fruit of the Spirit, below:
    a.
    b.
    c.
    d.
    e.

14. Would you hire the man in the illustration on page 54 in the text? Why or why not?

15. It is God who _____ the _____.

CHAPTER 5

YOUR MISSION STATEMENT

Here at the Bread of Life Ministries as should be with all churches and Para-ministries, we have clearly stated mission statements. In Matthew 5:13-14, Jesus made two of His most penetrating statements to those who follow Him; than you can find anywhere in Scripture. He said, *"You are the salt of the earth"* and *"You are the light of the world."* In these two statements Jesus gave us our perfect mission. They carry a tremendous amount of responsibility; require a lot of courage and determination [the narrow way]. These mission statements should cause us to realize what a grand and glorious privilege it is to be a child of the King.

America is experiencing a dark, dark period and Christians are the only people through whom God can send [light] and put flavor [salt] to make America palatable again. As Christians we have the truth and understanding [light] needed to help, and show people the "narrow way" to life. It's best for us to perhaps illustrate this by seeing ourselves as moons. Science has shown us that the moon actually has no light of its own; yet it shines! However, all of the light necessary for it to shine is reflected from the sun. The same is true of Christians. Though we have no light in ourselves, we shine with the light reflected from the Son within us. Keep shaking [salt] and shining [light]! These are and have been the mission statements for every Christian since Pentecost!

We hear much these days concerning the separation of church and state. Most of it is a scheme of Satan inflated by the media. The idea being put forth is intended to convince Christians to function only within the four walls [in private] and definitely not in the public square or marketplace. Many Christians believe this deception through biblical ignorance and have fallen silent, when outside of the home or church building. The world is crying enough is enough! And people are seeking relief and deliverance. They want life! Satan knows that Christ through the saints is their only hope! In fact! Through Christ, Christians are the only hope for America.

As a young preacher, I was blessed to preach in many revivals. One thing really impacted me; those communities that prayed and prepared for revival reaped a harvest. These communities participated in what was called "Revival Season" in the old days they were similar to the cowboys' round up time. Instead of rounding up cattle those old saints [salt and light] of the community rounded up sinners. The crops had been harvested and the revival rounded out the season's harvests. I remember my mother and others who went out in teams visiting families, church members who strayed, and strangers, all after a season of corporate mid-day prayer meetings.

As a boy I learned having participated in some meetings as a junior deacon that the visitations and fervent prayer meetings won the majority of the souls to Christ; so the revival services [preaching] were renewal for older members and salvation station for the new. Oh! What a time!

We must all learn to live together as brothers or we will perish together as fools.
– Martin Luther King Jr.

Many individuals in our churches today are fragments of a family. It might be the mother or father, a son or daughter, but fewer whole families together. It is not uncommon to find cases where some family members are attracted to a different denomination, non-denomination or to a different faith altogether. Can you imagine a family member who can live peaceably without striving to win their siblings or parents to Christ? As an advocate for the house church concept which is on the rise in this country today, I believe it is another element of God's plan of restoration. After sixteen years of planting churches and helping equip others through a Bible Institute that I co-founded with my Magdalene; I believe we know a little something that can get some of our traditional and institutional churches back on the evangelistic track.

One helpful concept is through establishing small group ministry with a full gospel flavor. A number of these churches have a large congregation, but on Wednesday night only a faithful few attend whatever services may be offered. Many local churches are maintaining the old Reformation concept of ministry and to some of them to maintain that traditional concept is more important than being concerned with changes for any reason! A major motivation for the Reformation was to get the **truth of God's Word** into the hands of the people at the lowest level. The question today is who will teach the teacher? Rather than teaching and developing leaders for small groups in many of our churches, the leaders fear losing their positions or some authority. It seems that many pastors or leaders think it best to leave the people to lean upon their own understanding of truth (see Proverbs 3:5-6). God forbid! How important is the truth of God's Word in your church?

How the Kingdom of God works

A man who won't die for something is not fit to live.
– Martin Luther King Jr.

Jesus used a parable of a farmer sowing seed to illustrate how the Word which is represented by the seed is sown (see Mark 4:14-20). The actual purpose of the parable is to show how the Kingdom of God works – through the Word of God. The Kingdom of God which encompasses the Christian's life, victories, and total spirituality is as simple as *taking the Word of God* and *sowing it* in your heart, caring for it and letting it germinate which will result in necessary and effective change. Like the seed, the Word of God has the power within to reproduce itself. However, for the process to work requires tilling the ground, planting the seeds, and watering the seeds. If you exclude either of the steps the seed will not germinate and produce fruit in your life. Many Christians are searching for answers to life's questions and drawing a blank to many of the responses they receive from their peers. I read an article about some excavators finding some corn seeds in an Egyptian pyramid that had been closed for 3000 years. They removed the seeds and planted them in the ground. The seeds germinated and produced a crop after lying dormant for 3000 years. They no doubt could have laid there another 1000 years producing absolutely nothing because they were not planted – just kept! Scientific research has revealed the fact that scientists can construct synthetic seeds which are authentic looking in every aspect except one – the seeds have no power to reproduce themselves as the authentic seeds have. That principle holds true for the human heart. The Word [the seed] must be planted in our hearts [good ground] in order to germinate and reproduce the blessings below:

- It is by the foolishness of preaching the gospel people are saved (see 1 Corinthians 1:21).
- It is through the Word of God that we are cleansed (see John 17:17).
- It is by the Word of God that we are healed of sickness and diseases (see Isaiah 53:4-5; Matthew 8:16-17).
- It is the Word of God that sustains our lives (see Proverbs 4:22).
- It is the Word of God that grows us into mature saints of God (see Ephesians 4:15).
- It is the Word of God that comforts, give peace and stability when it seems like your living might be in vain (see II Corinthians 15:3, 4).

Satan enjoys seeing any situation individually or corporately wherein we do not prioritize the teaching of the inerrant Word of God [the Bible] and it's being trusted by the people of God over all other considerations! Think about it all disciplines find the history of their beginning in the Bible. If there is a situation, need, or circumstance in your life of which you are seeking the **truth,** go back to the Bible. Is there a promise from the Lord concerning your situation? Plant the promise by faith in your heart and meditate on it. Oh! Praise God, there's the answer! The Scripture says that written promise is part of our inheritance – receive it!

*"Remember the former things of old, for I **am** God, and there is none like Me, declaring the end from the beginning, and from ancient times **things** that are not **yet** done, saying, My counsel shall stand, and I will do all My pleasure"* (Isaiah 46:9-10).

What you are [salt]

Jesus said, *"You are the salt of the earth."* Salt is one of the most stable compounds on the planet. It is effective only as long as it is pure. It never loses its saltiness on its own, but becomes ineffective when it is contaminated. Contamination happens when salt becomes mixed with some other chemical or foreign material.

Salt must be **kept** pure. When it is kept in its pure condition it only takes a small amount to accomplish its purpose of making food palatable by adding flavor or to preserve. Contamination happens if:

- We begin to walk too close to the world.
- We begin to mix with the worlds standards.
- We begin to handle the world's things.

The same principle works for those true to God:

- When we remain pure.
- When we are pure, it only takes a few of us to effect enormous change.
- When we are different and remain so.
- When we separate ourselves from the world.

By attempting to mix the standards of the world with God's standards, individually and corporately we become contaminated and lose our saltiness! The media and all the other allies of Satan are striving to make the saints of God think of themselves as grasshoppers; while they project themselves as giants.

Those who fall for this deception forfeit their effectiveness and Christian influence; however those who remain faithful to the narrow way can accomplish much through Christ who strengthens us. In 2 Corinthians 6:14-18, the Apostle Paul admonishes all Christians:

Do not be unequally yoked together with unbelievers. For what fellowship has righteousness with lawlessness? And what communion has light with darkness? And what accord has Christ with Belial? Or what part has a believer with an unbeliever? And what agreement has the temple of God with idols? For you are the temple of the living God. As God has said:

> *"I will dwell in them*
> *And walk among them*
> *I will be their God,*
> *And they shall be My people."*

Therefore;

> *Come out from among them*
> *And be separate, says the Lord.*
> *Do not touch what is unclean,*
> *And I will receive you."*
> *"I will be a Father to you,*
> *And you shall be My sons and*
> *daughters, says the Lord Almighty."*

Paul was not encouraging them to isolate themselves from unbelievers, but discouraging **compromise** and **accommodation** with the world's sinful values and practices.

He was encouraging the church (and the church today) to maintain integrity in the world just as Christ did. God promises them favor and protection. He exhorted the Corinthians to cleanse themselves from all filthiness; referring to their attitudes and actions that came from having false teachers walking and working among them.

I covered the secular humanists and religionists in the last chapter, much of the deception and confusion in the churches today comes from their messages being welcomed through the secular media and placed above the truths of God's Word. It is imperative that we understand our mission and what it incurs to be "the salt of the earth!" We must preserve the good.

What you do [light]

The second part of Jesus' mission statement that Christians **"are the light of the world."** This being fact, then the world is living in a state of darkness, even though they make proud claims of their own enlightenment. There are many Scriptures with which this truth is validated:

"He has delivered us from the power of darkness and conveyed us into the kingdom of the Son of His love" Colossians 1:13).

"For you were in darkness, but now you are light in the Lord. Walk as children of light" (Ephesians 5:8).

> *"But you are a chosen generation,*
> *A* royal ***priesthood**, a holy nation,*
> *His own special people,*
> *that you may proclaim*
> *the praises of Him*
> *who called you out of darkness*
> *into the marvelous light"* (1 Peter 2:9).

Only true Christians have been brought into the light
– the people of the world live in darkness.

The world does not recognize the darkness they are in. Martin Luther King Jr. said, *"Only when it is dark enough, can you see the stars."* The world is convinced of its own enlightenment. Their secular belief is *"knowledge brings light."* Please note, the secularists and religionists have **replaced** God's revelation with man's reasoning, **placing human insight above God's revealed wisdom and truth.** They have turned away from truth.

This deception is rapidly spreading among Christians as many of them embrace the lie that in the fall; man fell in his total being with the exception of his or her mind. Many people are **turning from the truth** and replacing the worship of God with the worship of their own intellect!

I would venture to say, I believe the majority of the people in the world think that all we need to solve all of our problems is more knowledge.

Adding a little to what I said about this subject in an earlier section. Humankind does not realize that **our** knowledge has only increased our *understanding of* **things** *[all of which are temporal/ earthy].*

The disciplines of science, philosophy, etc. to which we add business, commerce, and pleasure certainly do not add one iota of a peaceful life. The present NSA debacle is a good example. We have more knowledge than we know what to do with. We still can't get along as people or nations. It seems the only way out for many intellectuals remain to be suicide.

According to Jesus Himself, "Only Christians can be depositories of the light and life of Jesus Christ.

Then Jesus spoke to them again saying,
"I am the light of the world.
He who* follows *Me
shall not walk in darkness,
but have the light of life" (John 8:12).

The word "follows" conveys the idea of someone who gives him or herself completely to the person followed. Jesus had no half-hearted followers in mind when He spoke this. (Study also Matthew 8:18-22; 10:38-39). Jesus is God in the flesh. When a person is born again into His spiritual Kingdom, the Spirit of Jesus Christ is born into that person and the Holy Spirit begins to live in and through that individual.

Do you not know
that you are
the temple of God
and
that the Spirit of God
dwells in you?"
(1 Corinthians 3:16).

Our Place of Worship

Much confusion exists in Christian communities of faith in reference to the place of worship. Around the world, we find magnificent buildings constructed especially for and consecrated as "the house of God." This concept is totally foreign to the New Testament, which is the believer's sole authority in the matter of worship, or any other matter on which it speaks.

The woman of Samaria was confused regarding the matter of the correct geographical location for worship. "Our fathers worshipped in this mountain; (Mt. Gerizim); and you Jews say that in "Jerusalem is the place where one ought to worship"(John 4:20). Our Lord's reply to her makes perfectly clear that the geographical situation, or the kind of building, is totally *immaterial* to worship. Jesus said to her, "Woman believe Me, the hour is coming when you will neither on this mountain, nor in Jerusalem, worship the Father. You worship what you do not know; we know what we worship, for salvation is of the Jews.

But the hour is coming, and now is, when the true worshippers will worship the Father in spirit and truth; for the Father is seeking such to worship Him" (vv. 21-23). Jesus completely did away with one of the main draws for some preachers. The popular idea that one location or one building is more sacred than another; or that worship is more acceptable to Him when offered in one place over another. The place, or the building, has nothing whatever to do with worship. It is the *spiritual condition* of the worshipper.

Once the believer has fully grasped that fact – it will deliver him or her once and for all from the *misconception* regarding this matter. In America we are programmed for "greatness" be it size or number, the greater number or size, the more acceptable *you* are, to whom? Again, it is the spiritual condition of the worshipper, and not his or her physical location or surroundings that determines whether or not your worship is acceptable to the Father. The Christian worships, spiritually, where his or her great high Priest is. This is heaven or the holiest of all. Notice the illustration of the Tabernacle as the "pattern of things in the heavens." The writer goes on to describe how Aaron, Israel's high priest entered once a year into the holiest of all with the blood of the sin offering which he had offered for his own sins, and also for the sins of the people of Israel (Hebrews 9:1-10).

He then proceeds to contrast Aaron's high priestly work with that of Christ, the great High Priest. He says, "But Christ, being come a High Priest of good things to come, by a greater and more perfect tabernacle, not made with hands, that is to say not of this building; neither by the blood of goats and calves, but by His own blood, entered in once (for all) into the holy place, having obtained *eternal redemption for us*" (Hebrews (9:11-12). As the holiest of all, in the tabernacle, was a type of heaven and the presence of God; so Christ, by virtue of His substitutionary sacrifice, and the eternal value of His precious blood, He entered into heaven as the great High Priest of His redeemed people. "For Christ is not entered into the holy place made with hands, which are the figures (or types) of the true, but into heaven itself, now to appear in the presence of God for us" (Hebrews 9:23).

Not only has Christ entered into heaven as our Divine Representative, but He opened up, for all His people, *"a new and living way,"* by which they are *enabled spiritually* to enter the holiest also to pour out worship in the presence of God. The Word of God says, "Having therefore brethren, boldness to enter into the holiest by the blood of Jesus, by a new and living way, which He has consecrated for us through the veil, that is to say His flesh; and having an High Priest over the house of God, let us draw near, with a true heart, in full assurance of faith" (see Hebrews 10:19-22). Thus *every born again believer, being constituted a priest unto God* – is both spiritually and divinely invited to come by faith into the very Holiest of all and worship. What is true of an individual is also true of an assembly of believers. As they meet in the name of the Lord Jesus Christ, they form a God-constituted company of priests. As such, through their great High Priest, they may lay hold, *by faith, upon God's provision and spiritually enter the Holiest of all,* to present their worship to the Father and the Son.[30] This Christian hymn expresses this truth beautifully,

"The veil is rent, lo Jesus stands
Before the throne of grace;
And clouds of incense from His hands
Fill all that glorious place.
His precious blood is sprinkled there,
Before and on the throne;
And His own wounds in heaven declare

The work that saves is done.
Within the holiest of all,
Cleansed by His precious blood,
Before the throne we prostrate fall,
And worship Thee, our God." By J. G. Deck[31]

Christians are not the light of the world because of who we are –
but because of who Jesus is and what He has done! Praise God!

STUDY GUIDE: CHAPTER 5

1. Jesus gave the Christian two mission statements _____ and _____.

2. This has been the mission of every Christian since _____.

3. A major motivation of the _____ was to get the _____ into the hands of the people.

4. Salt must be kept _____.

5. Only _____ have been brought into the _____.

6. The word "follow" conveys the idea of _____ _____.

7. Jesus is _____ in the flesh.

8. We are _____ of Jesus Christ.

9. What happens when we mix the standards of the world with God's standards _____?

10. He has delivered you from the _____.

11. For many _____ the only way out is _____.

12. The moon receives its light from the _____ and Christians receive theirs from the _____.

13. The Christian worships, spiritually where his or her _____ _____ is.

14. The earthly tabernacle is a _____ of things in heaven.

15. Every born again believer is _____ a _____ priest of God.

CHAPTER 6

TO BE OR NOT TO BE

While attending Bible College in the early seventies, little was said concerning the United States in prophecy. Some have determined this country has no place in prophecy, and others say the United States would probably be a part of the Antichrist's army at Armageddon. However, in these last days unless we are prayerfully careful this nation may be totally insignificant on the world scene by then. Certainly a few years ago, very few people actually thought America would possibly take this broad path – even though clouds were appearing on the horizon. At that time the nation enjoyed a biblical worldview and Christian consensus. Today, the biblical worldview is being replaced with secular humanisms' atheistic worldview; and battle lines are clearly drawn. Unless we repent and turn back to God, the fate of this nation is sealed. God has clearly spoken of the eternal destiny of the "wicked and those nations that forget or turn their backs on Him" (see Psalm 9:17).

I've pointed out several times, America's assignment as God's depository of Christianity for the past three hundred years. My wife and I have had the privilege of observing and participating in Christian churches on four different continents and can say without a doubt, in America the freedom of worship and witness for the Christian is unmatched anywhere in the world! However, like anything else that we receive without struggle, there is little practical appreciation. Many of the people speaking in the name of Christianity and the Church have wrong motives; thus the cause of Christ is often greatly hindered or improperly represented before the world.

War on the Saints [First Beast]

Most of our teaching after Revelation 4:1 places the church with the Lord in heaven. Those things prophesied about Antichrist are future and true, however, Satan has definitely seems to have loosed the spirit of antichrist on America in the meantime. In Revelation 13:7, the Apostle John says,

*"It was granted to him [the Antichrist] to make war with the saints and to **overcome them**. And authority was given him over every tribe, tongue, and nation."*

Since prophecy is given a near and a far fulfillment, I believe the present day apostasy is possibly the near fulfillment in these last days. The word **overcome** in this passage reminds us that this word also means to **conquer,** defeat, or subdue – but not obliterate or eliminate. Christ **conquered** Satan at Calvary, but He did not eliminate him from the human experience, yet! Satan has been using secular humanism and religious Christianity for more than a hundred years to conquer the society and deceive the saints in America. His demonic workers have intensified immensely over the past thirty years.

John is prophesying that this antichrist spirit will have the power to overcome or conquer Christians *by keeping them from walking in the power of the Holy Spirit.* The Holy Spirit is the power source for Christians individually and corporately, enabling them to live and function *victoriously in Christ.* However when a society lives under the influence of the antichrist spirit, if not checked – that spirit will overcome them. We are experiencing such a scene here in America and the entire western civilization today. Unless the child of God is "built up in the most holy faith through the Holy Spirit and the truths of God's Word, they will be defeated! Many of the churches sad to say are in denial of this satanic assault. Like the secular humanists, many of the people in the churches of America really do not believe in the supernatural! This stealthy maneuver is having a death-defying effect on the spirituality of the Churches. Some time ago the Reverend Billy Graham reporting from his research, stated that 90% of the Christians in America are living defeated lives.

This is indicative of Christians trying to live and work through their trials and circumstances in their own strength. The quality of the life of a believer is determined by their spirituality. What may appear to be a sincere believer may in reality be a "show in the flesh" and as such, an abomination in the sight of God. The Apostle Paul divides all of humanity into three distinct classes:

1. Natural – Those persons who are by nature unregenerate; and therefore incapable of understanding the things of God.
2. Spiritual – Those persons who have been born from above, and indwelt by the Holy Spirit; consequently they possess the capacity for discerning and appreciating divine truth. This person also seeks to live a life pleasing to God.
3. Carnal – Those persons who though born from above and indwelt with the Spirit of God, live their life on earth in the power of the flesh instead of the power of the Holy Spirit.

There were many carnal believers in the church at Corinth and Paul had to say to them, "I ..... could not speak unto you as unto spiritual, but as unto carnal, even as unto babes in Christ ..... for you are yet carnal." (Study 1 Corinthians 2:14-3:2).

He is drawing attention to characteristics of carnality in them.

*   First, they were not spiritual [no power].
*   Second, they were not enjoying the divine fruit of the Spirit [Christlike character].

As born again Christians we know from the Scriptures and personal experience that it is impossible to live in the power of the flesh to try do so, means we are defeated even before we begin. We are to live full of the Spirit and according to His power and the Word of God [daily].

Many Christians tend to forget that our spiritual survivability depends on our daily intake of the Word of God, just as our physical bodies depend upon our daily intake of physical food. In 1 Corinthians 11:23-30, we see the how carnality greatly hinders the spiritual growth and worship:

*   Their worship is from the soul.
*   They grieve, quench and limit the Holy Spirit's ministry.
*   Carnal Christians make the atmosphere cold and clammy with a spirit of formalism.

Earlier I stressed how gifts and talents have supplanted the fruit of the Spirit on priority list of a great percentage of Christians today. The reason this is happening is that gifts are given; but the fruit has to be developed over time. Proper development of good fruit requires much care, time, and work for [spiritual growth and bearing fruit]. As I stated in an earlier section, the fruit is produced by the Holy Spirit and; the Word of God in mature Christians confirms this.

Satan's secular humanism has become embedded in key areas of society and has greatly influenced the unhealthy path the culture and wider society are so rapidly taking. As planned by Satan, this action is definitely influencing and affecting the spiritual walk of many Christians. He is orchestrating this through the [secular-driven] societal pressures outside; and religious Christianity [legalism] inside the church which denies the power of the Holy Spirit.

The Spiritless church is causing many Christians to lose sight of what it means to be committed and faithful to Christ. It also denies the possibility of living a supernatural life of victory in Christ.

The majority of Christians have become proficient in knowing what to say in Christian circles making it seem that we are devoted – but our actions and fruitlessness boldly expose our weaknesses of assimilation and accommodation to the antichrist spirit in the world.

A strategy practiced on the field of battle is to wound the enemy soldiers rather than kill them. One wounded soldier requires two soldiers be pulled out of battle to carry and care for him. Satan is using that strategy in some aspects – he can't kill the Christians, but he just wounds their reputation and testimony making them ineffective as the presence of Christ in the world.

Prepared for the Offense

In Ephesians 1:1, 16-19, the Apostle Paul prayed a prayer for the Gentiles, as the prisoner of Jesus Christ for them. He continues on his knees, *"For this reason I bow my knees"* (v. 1). His purpose for praying to the Father is for **all** believers in heaven and earth. Note his seven petitions:

1. That the Father would give you the Spirit of wisdom (v. 17).
2. That He may give you revelation in the knowledge of Him (v. 17).
3. That the eyes of your understanding be enlightened (v. 18).
4. That you may know what is the hope of His calling (v. 18).
5. That you may know what is the riches of the glory of his inheritance in the saints (v. 18).
6. That you may know the exceeding greatness of His power to us-ward (v. 19).
7. That you may know and be filled with all the fullness of God; and you experience all aspects of His truth and power (v. 19).

Christians will possess godly knowledge and insight of which a sanctified [renewed] mind is capable (Study Romans 12:1-6). A spiritually enlightened mind is the only means of truly understanding and appreciating the hope and inheritance we have in Christ; as we **live obediently** for Him.

The reason Satan is able to successfully wreak havoc upon Christians is because so many lack biblical knowledge without which we will never realize the power and riches we have in Christ Jesus. Read his prayer for all Christians again below:

"That the eyes of your understanding being enlightened; that you may ***know*** *what is the hope of His calling what are the riches of the glory of His inheritance in the saints and what is the exceeding greatness of* ***His power*** *toward us who believe, according to the working of His mighty power."*

If we are going to counter Satan's current attack against America; those of us who believe and embrace these promises must walk and act in the power of the Holy Spirit. It is far later than we think!

How can we **know** we are walking in the power of the Holy Spirit?

- We **have** victory over sin!
- We are **bearing** the fruit and characteristics of Christ through the power of the Holy Spirit!

- We **will** be able to stand!

> *"But the Lord is faithful,*
> *who will establish you*
> *and guard you*
> *from the evil one"*
> (2 Thessalonians 3:10).

The greatest turning point

In recent history we have witnessed numerous turning points in the world. They ranged for example the turning point of Dr. Martin Luther King Jr. and the Civil Rights Movement, Katrina, political and economic turning points, and now the Apostle Paul prophecies in II Timothy 3:1-5 how Christians will be overcome or conquered in the last days and marked by being. **"But know this, that in the last days perilous times will come. For men [human beings] will be:**

- Lovers of themselves
- Lovers of money
- Boasters
- Proud
- Blasphemers
- Disobedient to parents
- Ungrateful
- Unholy (immoral)
- Without love
- Unforgiving
- Slanderous
- Without self-control
- Brutal
- Not lovers of the good
- Traitors
- Headstrong
- Haughty
- Lovers of pleasure rather than lovers of God
- Having a form of godliness but denying the power

Paul admonished the church and the true Christians to **have nothing** to do with them" (see II Timothy 3:1-5). Like Jesus, we invite people to come to Him just as they are – however they are **not** to remain as they are! He saw this day that we are presently living in America. He called it terrible times! Why? Because the characteristics he saw [listed above] would be prevalent among Christians today. He is not saying that every Christian will display the characteristics of our old sinful nature – *but we will continue to demonstrate some of them. One is too many!* What does that mean? In witness to what Dr. Billy Graham reported, it means we have allowed Christians to possess these characteristics, mainly through assimilation by allowing these people to remain in the Christian community. Many of them have no intention of changing as stated in an earlier section.

I read an illustration wherein a man had climbed high up on a bridge with the intention of committing suicide; when the police arrived the captain sent a young officer up to talk the man down. The police captain looked away in conversation for a minute to answer a question.

He glanced back up on the bridge and both men were gone. Somehow the man talked the young officer into jumping with him. We are in the greatest turning point as Satan through secular humanism and religious Christianity deceives people, even some Christians by suggesting that the broad way is the best way; and like the young policeman on the bridge:

1. Many are denying the power of the Holy Spirit that is given to all who believe to overcome our sinful nature.
2. Many are living defeated lives in the absence of the Spirit, and without the Word and prayer in their lives. Religious Christianity [legalism] has convinced many Christians that church work in their own natural strength and abilities will get them to heaven.
3. Many have been duped by the the spirit of this age, who has supernaturally overcome them.

The fruit of our society reveal that the majority of our people have been very subtly deceived into submission. However, within the 10% of undefeated Christians in Dr. Graham's research there is a group that is **impossible to deceive!** These are those Christians who allow the Holy Spirit and the truth of God's Word to transform them into fruitful, mature disciples in Christ – basic training for all disciples (see Matthew 24:24).

Give yourself away – the more of yourself you spend the more you gain!

In chapter 2 the Apostle Paul exhorts the saints to endure hardship, be diligent, rightly divide the Word, and be vessels fit for the Master's use even in the context of difficult, and perilous times. This does not mean these saints have arrived; it means they are on the way – **the narrow way!** The narrow way again, means separation and obedience unto God's will, God's way, through God's Spirit and His Word.

The Cultural War [False Prophet]

Periodically on a newscast some world leader or politician will be heard speaking of the world as one community [global**ism**]. In many quarters religious leaders have been speaking for years of one world religion [ecumen**ism**] and here again under one leader. Looking again at Revelation 13, we are introduced to the second beast. The Apostle John reports,

*"Then I saw another beast coming up out of the earth, and he had two horns **like a lamb and spoke like dragon"** (v.11).*

As with the prophecy of the Antichrist, there is a near and far fulfillment. Think about it, **a beast that looks like a lamb, but speaks like a dragon!** The spirit of antichrist is corrupting and secularizing the society; so the false prophet will corrupt and secularize the religious atmosphere and culture, specifically teaching false values. He appears harmless, **like a lamb** but represents the perverted values that accompany the Antichrist and – speaks **like a dragon.** Wake up saints! From John's prophecy he has the appearance of a pseudo prophet, proclaiming *godly* concerns while teaching false values about spiritual matter and biblical standards.

An honest look at many of our judges and politicians reveals this ungodly deception has almost eliminated *"We the people."* Public opinion determines much of our judicial and political decisions even though many of them violate the moral laws of God.

We are engaged in a cultural war being fought for the hearts, minds, wills, affections [**souls**] and life styles of the people. Occupying center position in the war are the government, academia and the media all of which have been fully secularized. Having already dethroned our Christian consensus and biblical worldview, each of the three has their own agenda in the war against God's moral law, the church, saints and authentic Christianity. The expansion of the media has allowed America to impact the world with our individualistic, humanistic and immoral lifestyles. It's important that we understand their ungodly worldview is by choice. The Scripture distinctly tells us,

*"Because, although **they knew God,** they did not glorify Him as God, nor were they thankful, but became futile in their thoughts, and their foolish hearts were darkened, professing to be wise, they became fools, and changed the glory of the incorruptible God into an image made like corruptible man – and birds and four-footed animals and creeping things"*(Romans 1:20-23).

They knew, that is, God has shown them the truth about Himself through creation. (see v. 18) Yet, even with all this evidence in creation, people still refuse to recognize their Creator, worship and glorify Him as God.

The Media

Movies and television sitcoms romanticize cohabitation, lewd and explicit open heterosexual acts and now they are joined by homosexual and lesbian acts all over the media landscape. The secular humanism agenda guided by **government, education, secular media and public opinion** has changed the way we:[32]

- Think – saying the same thing the world is saying on the specific issues.
- Worship – many forms (about me/ us) and not toward God.

- Determine what matters *most?* – (me and mine) happiness, good feelings and entertainment.
- Raise our families – while allowing top priority to the secular media, school, and peer pressure in shaping our children over parental training in the truths of God's Word.
- Operate our schools – by allowing secular humanism and multiculturalism to replace Christian influence and the biblical worldview.
- Run our government – through special interest groups.
- Do politics – obey religious Christianity, secular public opinion and the elite 1%.
- Set our moral standards – based on the secular humanism agenda.
- Establish our social order – again according to the secular humanism agenda.
- View the Christians and Christianity – as obsolete and replaced by the secular humanists and religionists.
- View the secular worldview – above the biblical worldview.
- View human beings – as animals [rather than created in the image of God].
- View life and death – live life to the fullest getting all of the things you can, because when you die it's all over. You no longer exist. God forbid!
- View Christianity and the Word of God as human inventions.
- View the Bible as an uninspired and fallible history book.

Self-centeredness

Another worldly influence in fact, one of the strongest to invade the church has been aimed at getting Christians to become self-centered. The deception is to get us to change our focus standards from Christ-centeredness to self-centeredness and serve ourselves:

- self-love
- self-interest
- self-satisfaction
- self-gratification

The Scriptures speak of those who do not want to retain God in their knowledge! Our society is dangerously rushing headlong in that direction. This has caused Christians to be more tolerant of and indifferent to many sins described in the Bible as abominations to God; that are now becoming ok and common in the culture. Those sins that were permissible by worldly standards in our society thirty or forty years ago, but "unthinkable" publically are now being tolerated and assimilated in the society as normal and even affecting some attitudes in the Christian communities:

- Personal accountability, respect for God, others, authority, and self-control are now obsolete according to humanistic thinking.
- Nothing is indecent.
- Rules and boundaries are to be fought against.
- Very little is to be honored or respected.

New Tolerance

We are told that everyone should recognize the secularly introduced "new" tolerance which promotes:

- Supplanting the spiritual values and biblical way of thinking with the humanistic values and way of thinking.
- Immoral causes and ungodly standards on issues
- Safe sex over abstinence
- Outlaw prayer in the public
- Abortions
- Multiple Divorces
- Multiple Marriages
- Same-sex marriages and co-habitation
- Teaching homosexuality as an acceptable life style in school
- The destruction of Christianity and the Bible
- Secular humanism's no God
- Evolution is being taught as truth
- Human beings are animals and therefore are not accountable for behavior and conduct unbecoming of a human being – as long as no one is hurt?
- The right not to be offended

- No absolute truth
- Establish your own truth
- Man is his own god
- No supernatural[33]

Webster's dictionary defines **tolerate** as "recognize and respect (others' beliefs, practices, etc) *without sharing them,"* and to bear or put up with (someone or something not especially liked). The Apostle Paul expresses this attitude:

"……….. bears all things …….. endures all things" (1 Corinthians 13:7).

The Bible also tells us to, "Live in harmony with one another. If it is possible, as far as it depends on you, live in peace with everyone" (see Romans 15:7). The Bible distinctly tells us how as Christians we are to act toward each other (not just to strong but all Christians) and serve not only Christians in love, but also do good to those outside of the faith (Study Ephesians 4:2, 32; Colossians 3:13; Galatians 6:10).

The Christian consensus was born out of the traditional tolerance defined above. However, with the demise of the Christian consensus in America, the word "tolerate" has been re-defined.

Secular humanism has redefined it to mean that all beliefs, values, lifestyles, and perceptions of truth are equal." This means there is no hierarchy of truth; your beliefs and my beliefs are equal – and **all** truth is relative. Do you believe that? Our children are being taught in school to believe that! It equates to all truths, all values, and all lifestyles are equal! The teaching of the "new tolerance" determines that what every *individual* believes or say is equally *right* and *equally valid.* But they are not![34]

Public Education

Humanistic thinking has conquered public education at all levels. Secular humanism (thought) claims not to be a religion; therefore they can set man up as his own god. Christian influence is no longer incorporated into our textbooks, nor can it be taught in public schools. However, nearly every textbook has multiculturalism and secular humanism influence inserted throughout.

Secular humanists know that if they control [and for the most part they do] what our young people are taught and what they see, hear, think **and believe** – they can [and do] determine our society's philosophical standards. I heard on the news recently of a school being sued by an atheistic group because they allowed a group of Christian teens to meet in one of the rooms. The school is now under the gun for bowing to the atheists. However, the school had to repent after realizing that a law was passed in 1989 which prohibits any interference with the assembly of the Christian groups and their rights and privileges are the same as the non-Christian groups who meet there. This is the reason our Christian heritage, has been extracted from all curriculums and school activities.

We are seeing come true what President Abraham Lincoln said:

"The philosophy of the classroom today will be the philosophy of the government tomorrow."   – Abraham Lincoln

---

Are you concerned! Does it bother you that the moral standards of American society have deteriorated much more in this last generation than in all of the previous years combined since the nation's founding? The spiritual foundation of our nation is being torn apart and yet **the majority** of the people *including many Christians* do not seem to be concerned until they are personally affected.

In Hosea 4:6 we are told, "My people are *destroyed* for a lack of knowledge." The *failure* of Israel's religious leaders which included some of the prophets failed to teach God's law to the people (see Malachi 2:7). The lack of knowledge brought about their *downfall*. Instead of being shook up about it, there is a cry for greater freedom to feed their sinful nature! Satan's devious plan seems to be working folks!

Assimilation

Jesus taught the principle of "salt" to illustrate the mission of Christians. If we assimilate anything other than the truth of God's Word by mixing with the impurities of the world, we will become contaminated and lose our ability to flavor and preserve. Webster's Dictionary defines the word, "assimilate" to mean – to come into conformity with the customs, attitudes, and take in as one's own. As Christians coming into assimilation with the world contaminates us. Here lies the *problem* for Christians!

Research shows that the Christians are conforming to the world at a very fast pace; which means Satan's deception is effective. Barna research reports 32% of unsaved believed God exists, but what's sad, is that's the same percentage among Christians. The question is what about the almost 75% of Christians that does not have a clear answer to this question?

The people of the world are naturally operating in line with current worldly thinking. That is exactly what we should expect from them since they don't know any better as *the world lives in darkness.*

Many Christians *have allowed the culture* to exchange their commitment to Christ and righteousness through assimilation. But we know better and must be careful that we don't succumb to the spirit of tolerance toward the world. The freedom people enjoy these days to openly talk about and display the most grievous sin; flaunting them publicly is a most deceptive form of dissimilation.

Our influence as salt and light in and on our society is dependent upon our being separated from – not identical with the world. It seems that very few Christians today are truthfully committed to our mission to be salt and light.

God's judgment comes – because of rejection of the truth of God's Word (see Romans 2:2; Psalm 81:12).

In Romans 1:21, the Apostle Paul explains this malady prevalent in societies of the last days. In America, rejection of God's truth is fast becoming the norm in all segments of our society as Satan turns up the heat realizing that he has but a short time. Notice the progressive states:

- Because that when they **knew** God:
- They did not glorify Him.
- Neither were they thankful.
- They did not want to retain God in their knowledge.

- They began to imagine foolish, wicked, and idolatrous thoughts in their hearts.
- Their heart became hardened and their spirit darkened.
- They profess to be wise, yet they became fools.
- Human beings became the object of their own worship.

God's Judgment

- God gave them up **(spirit)** to unclean lusts in their hearts v. 24.
- God gave them up **(body)** to vile affections v. 26.
- God gave them over **(soul)** to a reprobate mind (no longer experience convictions) v. 28.

The wrath of God is revealed from heaven against all ungodliness and unrighteousness of men [and women] (see Romans 2:2; Psalm 81:12).

What can we do?

The attitudes above can be curbed by understanding the general characteristics and needs of the various groups or generations targeted. The older generational Christians should have wisdom from God, along with their experiences and understanding of life to contribute. Then train the new leadership of the groups in the way that they should go. I believe the principles of Proverbs 22:6 can be applied to any age group of born again believers. Our training concentration should be to:

- Make sure they are rooted and grounded in the authentic gospel of Christ (salvation complete).
- Make sure they are rooted and grounded in authentic community (assimilated into the body of Christ).
- Make sure they are rooted and grounded in authentic transformation (growth to maturity).
- Make sure they are rooted and grounded in authentic missions (evangelism/ edification/ social justice).

This means that everyone is a "wanted person" – wanted by the Lord to be rescued from the *practice* of sin, delivered from the *power* of sin, and freed from the *pollution* of sin. In turn, the redeemed person is wanted as an instrument to win others to Christ, to *"Brighten Your Corner" where you are* and be a center of attraction to draw people to the narrow way, and spread a winsome influence for extending the Kingdom of God.

STUDY GUIDE: CHAPTER 6

1. America has been the _____ of Christianity for _____ years.

2. It was granted to him _____ to make war with the _____.

3. Explain below what is meant by a "renewed mind."

4. Many Christians lack _____ _____

5. How can we tell when we are walking in the Spirit:

6. Define globalism?

7. He appears _____ like a _____ but speaks like a _____.

8. The battle we are in is being fought for the _____ _____ of the people.

9. List five ungodly standards promoted by the new tolerance: _____ _____.

10. Humanistic thinking has conquered _____.

11. Secular humanism and multiculturalism has been _____ throughout the public school's textbook system.

12. Abraham Lincoln is credited with saying, "the philosophy of the _____ today will be the philosophy of the _____ tomorrow.

13. Barna research statistics reports _____% of unsaved persons surveyed believe God exists. Ironically the % for Christians is _____.

14. The wrath of God is revealed from heaven against all _____ and _____ of men and women.

15. We need _____ from God along with our own experiences and understanding of life.

SECTION III
I AM THE WAY

CHAPTER 7

TRANSFORMATION – THE NARROW WAY

When the people therefore saw that Jesus was not there, nor His disciples, they also got into boats and came to Capernaum, *seeking Jesus.* And when they found Him on the other side of the sea, they said to Him, "Rabbi, when did you come here?" Jesus answered them and said, "Most assuredly, I say to you, you *seek* Me, not because you saw the signs, but because **you ate of the loaves and were filled.** Do not labor for food which perishes, but for food which endures to **everlasting life,** which the **Son of Man** <u>will give you,</u> because God the Father has set His seal on Him."

Then they said to Him, "What shall we do, that we may work the works of God?" Jesus answered and said to them, *"This is the work of God that you believe in Him whom He sent."* Therefore they said to Him, "What sign will you perform then, that we may see it and believe You?" What work will You do? "Our fathers ate the manna in the desert, as it is written. *He gave them bread from heaven to eat."* Then Jesus said to them,

*"Most assuredly, I say to you, Moses did not give you the bread from heaven. For **the bread of God is He who comes down from heaven and gives life to the world."** Then they said to Him, "Lord, give us this bread always" (see John 6:24-34).

The Bread of Life

The people no doubt saw Jesus as a "miracle worker" who would supply their physical needs rather than spiritual needs forever [notice He gave them fish for one day only]. In their interpretation the people missed the truth, so Jesus corrected them. The manna had not come from Moses, but it had been provided by God. *Therefore, God is still the giver of* **true bread – that is, eternal life** (see v. 33). [Emphasis added throughout].

Jesus said, *"I am the bread of life."* So He is necessary to *us* for our food. In fact He is our food! He enables us to meet whatever life calls for to keep us in strength and health. For example: A man is tired; and because he's tired he is irritable and impossible. However, once he has a good sumptuous meal, he will become his old usual self. Why? Because the strength that was in the food has passed *into* him and has become his strength and made him stronger and a better man.

So *in* Christ there is food which feeds and strengthens; which sustains and restores spent vigor and vitality enabling us to do and to be what without Him is totally impossible! Many Christians are missing this fact and it shows up in their fruitless lives. So many read His word and then try in their own strength to apply it; not realizing His promise of power after the Holy Spirit has come upon us (see Acts 1:8). Apart from this, the needed power just isn't there! And all of the well-spent efforts to obey Christ's commands are hopeless, as a person trying to pick up the front end of his truck while someone else removes and replaces a flat tire. The Galileans now exclaim, **Lord give us this bread always** (v. 34). So we see Jesus in the first of the great I Am statements of the Gospel:

- I am the bread of life (v. 35).
- I am the living bread (v. 51).
- I am the bread which came down from heaven (v. 41).

Moses was a mighty servant of the Most High God. Yet "What Moses gave you was not the bread from heaven; it is My Father who gives you the *true* bread from heaven; and He is offering that to you *in* Me."

The Centrality of Christianity

Jesus is the centrality of Christianity because we find the revelation of God only in a *person*, Jesus Christ. We know about God – His character and passion through Jesus. This makes Christianity unique among the major religions of the world. But Christianity finds the initial revelation of God in a person. This does not make Christianity superior, but different. From John's gospel, in Jesus *"the Word became flesh and lived among us."*

This is the central meaning of our foundational doctrines of the faith and any faith without them is not true Christianity. Beginning with the *incarnation*: Jesus is *seen,* God embodied in a human body life. He is the revelation; the incarnation of what God is like and of what God is most passionate in His heart.

The interweaving of God, Jesus, the Holy Spirit and the Bible are the heart of the Christian revelatory vision; which leads to the finished work of Jesus on Calvary and to "seeing Jesus again." This image of Jesus results in emphasis of His identity, the Son of God, the "light of the world," the "bread of life," the promised Messiah who will come again. It emphasizes the significance of the redemptive salvation of grace in His death, the purpose for His coming; He died for our sins. While the emerging paradigm affirms the decisive centrality of Jesus – it sees Jesus quite differently than the earlier one does. All of which leads to the following declarations:

- He was miraculously born of a virgin.
- He is the Bread of life.
- He died for our sins and redeemed us through His shed blood.
- He physically resurrected from the grave.
- Thus Jesus is the only way of salvation.
- Jesus is the only way to God and heaven.
- Therefore Christianity is more than mere religion – it is life in right relationship with God, eternal life.
- Jesus knew and taught about Himself – and left His Spirit and a body of life instructions for us, in the Bible!

The New Birth

How to get to God today seems to depend upon who is telling it today. We hear one way and then we hear many ways. That is so sad many people enter eternity each day never knowing the truth.

Jesus was approached by Nichodemus, a ruler of the Jews, one of the Jew's highest religious leaders, who didn't have a clear answer. I'm sure that many who after having read the previous chapters may identify with Nichodemus. As they conversed Jesus told him "…. You must be born again ...." (John 3:3). So I'm saying none of the above is possible without **first, "you must be born again!"**

One of the shortcomings plaguing churches today is people being admitted to membership who are not truly born again. When we were born into the world we had one thing in common. No matter our pedigree, economics or social status; we were all born sinners. We all came short of the glory of God even in birth as a result of sin passed down from Adam and Eve to all humanity (see Romans 6:23; also study Genesis 1-3). Sin separated humanity from God's presence; however, before God created humans He already had a plan of reconciliation in place to reconcile sinners to Himself (see Genesis 3:15). When sin came it distorted the image of God in which humans were created. Human beings became depraved in all of their being. So in order for anyone to come into the presence of God they must experience a second birth. When man sinned he died spiritually; therefore all of their off springs would be born spiritually dead. Human beings are triune meaning they are three in one: spirit, soul, and body.

The Apostle Paul prayed concerning this **fallen** condition in all human beings, *"Now may the God of peace Himself sanctify your whole spirit, soul, and body be preserved blameless at the coming of our Lord Jesus Christ"* (1 Thessalonians 5:2). Paul admonishes us in the Scripture above that the goal of salvation [the new birth] is to bring the *whole* person back in right relationship with God. Paul continues, *"Not by works of righteousness which we have done, but according to His mercy He saved us, through the washing of regeneration and renewing of the Holy Spirit"* (Titus 3:5). Here we are taught that the Holy Spirit quicken or [gives new life] to people in regeneration, the new birth. In John 3:3-5, Jesus taught the same truth in His conversation with Nicodemus. Jesus answered and said unto him, *"Most assuredly, I say unto you, unless one is born again, he [or she] cannot see the kingdom of God. Nicodemus said to Him, "How can a man be born when he is old? Can he enter a second time into his mother's womb and be born again? Jesus answered, "most assuredly, I say to you unless one is born of water and the Spirit, he cannot enter the kingdom of God."*

Regeneration

The Holy Spirit draws us and convinces us through:

- The hearing the Gospel of Christ that we need Him, our Savior.
- The next step is to receive that truth and accept Jesus as your Savior in your heart and confess Him with your mouth.
- The Bible says you are saved or born again (see Romans 10:9-10). The Holy Spirit imparts [new spiritual life] into your now regenerated spirit.

In 1 Peter 1:23, the Apostle Peter explains how:

*"Having been born again, not of corruptible seed but incorruptible, through the **Word of God** which lives and abides forever."*

In James 1:18 we are told,

*"Of His own will He brought us forth by the **Word of truth**, that we might be a kind of firstfruits of His creatures."*

These passages clearly point out that it is the **Word of God** that the Holy Spirit uses in regeneration – but it is only as the Holy Spirit uses the Word that the new birth occurs.

In John 6:63, we are told, *"It is the Spirit who gives life; the flesh profits nothing. The words that I speak to you are spirit, and they are life.*

Regeneration begins as our spirit is quickened (made alive) by God through the Holy Spirit using the Word of God. As a result of the event we become a new creature *in Christ* and a partaker of God's divine nature (1Corinthians 1:30; 2 Peter 1:4). We are justified or made righteous (study carefully 2 Corinthians 5:17, 21). At this time we are reconciled to God by grace through faith in the finished work of our Lord and Savior, Jesus Christ [His death and resurrection]. (Isaiah 53:11; Romans 10:9-10; 14:16-17, 26).

Victory of the Cross

What is done with the convert at this point in regeneration is very important; and will impact the individual's destiny either positively or negatively. The question is often raised concerning baptism immediately following conversion. While there is not a particular problem with baptism immediately following conversion, there can be some major shortcomings, notice the various arguments, some:

- Make the argument catechesis needs to be complete before baptism.
- Encourage that it is okay if you have faith formation in place.
- Think baptism should not be rushed through because it is a one-time sacrament in the New Testament. The individual is making a commitment before God that is very serious.
- Believe there must be no reservations as to the authenticity of the conversion; and therefore more time for observation.
- Insist there needs to be a time of education, conscious reflection, and prayer.

I believe there has to be a period of clarification, biblical teaching and revelation of truth through the Spirit of God. I am a Bible teacher and my prayer for the students is that the Spirit will reveal the truth with understanding to them. This has to be a spirit and heart operation – more than head knowledge. The goal here is victory **in** Christ Jesus. The Scripture says,

*"But of Him you are **in Christ Jesus,** who became for us wisdom from God – and righteousness and sanctification and redemption – that, as it is written, **"He who glories, let him glory in the Lord"*** (1 Corinthians 1:30).

The truth to be gained here is we are in Christ. How did we get there? God put us there. "But of **Him,** you are in Christ." Not of your own efforts, nor is it the results of any plan we might have had. God did it! Regeneration is not of our own works, but by the Spirit through faith in the finished work of Jesus Christ.

Everything is made accessible **only** to us who are **in** Christ – His righteousness and His redemption. The Spirit reveals a picture of this truth of being ["in Christ"] in Hebrews 7:9-10, *Even Levi, who receives tithes, paid tithes through Abraham, so to speak, for he was still **in the loins** of his father when Melchizedek met him.* We see from these verses all Israel and Levi were in Abraham and we are in Christ. So when:

- When He died on the cross – we died in Him.
- When they buried Him – we were buried in Him.
- When He arose from the grave – we arose in Him (Study 2 Corinthians 5:15).
- When He was seated at the right hand of God – we were seated in Him.
- When He said, "He had all power" – we have all power in Him.

All by God's marvelous grace accessed through faith. To illustrate this: Suppose you put a dollar bill **in** you Bible. Wherever your Bible goes, the dollar goes because it is **in** the Bible. Bury your Bible on a shelf, that dollar is buried **in** it. When the Bible is retrieved from the shelf, so is the dollar bill in it. So is the believer in Christ upon Christ's resurrection. Jesus said to follow Him is difficult – but He did not say impossible. He gave us a Helper, the Holy Spirit.

Walk in the Spirit

The Holy Spirit now dwells in your spirit working from the inside out. He is transforming you into Christlikeness. Before the Spirit comes in, the soul [comprised of the mind, will, and affections] ruled because of our sin nature (see Genesis 1:26-28; 3:1). God's order is spirit, soul, and body; which is also the Spirit's order of spiritual transformation [sanctification].

Paul says, *"Now hope does not disappoint, because the love of God has been **poured out** in our hearts by the Holy Spirit **who was given** to you"* (Romans 5:5).

Please notice, we now have the love of God and the Holy Spirit in our hearts. Regeneration then is the impartation of a new nature, God's own nature – to those who are truly born again (see 2 Peter 1:4). Our renewed soul is a reflection of our new nature. Our mind which was blind is now opened to understanding the revealed truths of God's Word (see Romans 12:1-2; 1 Corinthians 13:1-8). Our will is in harmony with God's will (see John 4:34; 6:38; Galatians 1:10).

As we begin to practice our daily wisdom required disciplines: studying God's Word, prayer and meditation, our souls (mind, will and affections) are renewed. Our spiritual growth in Christ and commitment to Him in service are critically connected to our faithfulness to our daily disciplines. Some Christians become spiritual giants in a short period of time; while others remain spiritual dwarfs throughout their lives. While time is in the Lord's hands, we can hinder our own growth or progression in our sanctification and maturity through our thoughtless interruptions of God's plan for our individual and corporate lives (see Romans 6:12-14; 1 Peter 2:24-25; 4:1-2).

When your spirit has been born again [justification] – Christ has taken your sins and has given you His righteousness (see 2 Corinthians 5:21). The soul and body must be renewed through the Holy Spirit and revelation of the truths of God's Word. In sanctification we must be yielded to the Spirit and our will in God's will (see Romans 7:5-12; 12:1-5; Philippians 2:12-13; 3:7-11). The Apostle Paul admonishes,

"I beseech you therefore, brethren, by the mercies of God that you present your bodies a living sacrifice, holy, and acceptable to God, which is your reasonable service. And do not be conformed to this world, but be transformed by the renewing of your mind, that you may prove what is that good and acceptable and perfect will of God" (Romans 12:1-2).

Transformation for kingdom living and service begins with a "renewed mind." The mind is the conduit through which God works transformation (sanctification) and renewal of the soul and body.

"As a man [or woman] thinks in his [or her] heart, so is he [or she]" (see Proverbs 23:7; John 17:17). Brackets added.

We must begin to view reality from God's perspective. We love what God loves and hate what God hates. The Word of God is the key to the renewing of our minds. We hear the Word and receive it through our wills. Remembering the Word of God is "the Incorruptible Seed" (see 1 Peter 1:23), our willingness and receptiveness of that "Seed" indicates that we are "good ground." The seed grows in our spirit and cleanses (sanctifies our soul) from the inside out (see John 17:17; Hebrews 4:12).

The Word of God and the indwelling Spirit of God transform us holistically. Constant feeding of the spirit man through the study of the God's Word, meditation, prayer and application will brings us into spiritual maturity (sanctification and discipleship), the goal of regeneration. For we have the mind of Christ (1 Corinthians 2:16).

"There is therefore now no condemnation to those who are in Christ Jesus, who do not walk according to the flesh, but according to the Spirit" (Romans 8:1).

Normally the word "therefore" marks the conclusion of the verses immediately preceding it. But here it introduces the staggering results of the truth of Paul's teaching in the first seven chapters; the reconciliation is by faith alone on the basis of God's overwhelming grace. I will insert before going further, Romans 8 is one of the most beloved chapters in the Bible. It opens *"in Christ Jesus"* (v. 1); and it ends *"in Christ Jesus."* (v. 39) It is important to note all the promises in this chapter are ours *in Christ Jesus.* We step from chapter 7, which describes a believer battling with the flesh, to chapter 8, which *describes the spiritual man or woman in Christ Jesus.* For them there is no condemnation.

No condemnation – "condemnation" is used exclusively in judicial settings as the opposite of acquittal. It refers to a verdict of guilty and the penalty that the verdicts demand. Listen Now! No sin a true believer can commit past, present or future can be held against him or her since the penalty was paid by Christ and righteousness was imputed to the Christians *in Christ Jesus.* This individual does not walk according to the flesh or the five senses; but walks according to the Spirit through our 6th sense, faith (see Romans 8:4, 9-14).

The Spirit will keep you from falling

I say then: "Walk in the Spirit, and you shall not fulfill the lust of the flesh. For the flesh lusts against the Spirit and the Spirit against the flesh; and these are contrary to one another, so that you do not do the things you wish. But if you are led by the Spirit, you are not under the law" (Romans 5:16-18).

If we walk by the Holy Spirit, if we are led by the Spirit, if we yield ourselves to the Spirit, if we present our bodies a living sacrifice, holy acceptable unto God in the Holy Spirit and give the Holy Spirit right of way in our lives, He will give us victory over the flesh.

"Walk" refers to our lifestyles, our habits of living and thinking that characterize our lives (see Luke 1:6; Ephesians 4:17; 1 John 1:7). Our walk also expresses daily conduct, since every Christian is indwelt by the Holy Spirit, who has shed the love of God in our hearts, therefore will we manifest the fruit produced in our lives.

There is much spiritual ignorance among God's people concerning our relationship, as believers, to the Holy Spirit. I want to point out a few things concerning our relationship with Him:

- Every truly saved person who has received God's grace in Christ is born of the Holy Spirit [quickened in our spirit] and through His power becomes a child of God (see John 3:3-8; James 1:18; 1 Peter 1:22; 1 Peter 2:3).

- The moment a person is truly born again, that believer is baptized in the Holy Spirit into the body of Christ. The Lord Jesus Christ is the One who is the baptizer (see Matthew 3:11; Acts 1:5). Through the baptism of the Holy Spirit he or she becomes a member of the body of Christ (see 1 Corinthians 12:12-15, Ephesians 4:4; 5:30; also see the gift of the Holy Spirit in Acts 1:8; 2:38-39; John 14:17; 167-14).

- The moment the new birth is experienced, the true believer receives the Holy Spirit in his or her heart (see Romans 8:9, 14). The Holy Spirit is the unction, the anointing, and the teacher. He leads the believer day by day and guards us from the dangers of *apostasy* (see 1 John 1:18-27).

- Every truly born again believer is *sealed* by the Holy Spirit the moment he or she receives the new birth …. and is thus made God's son, sealed until the day of redemption when our Lord returns (see 1 Corinthians 1:21-22; Ephesians 1:13-14; 4:30).

- Every true born again believer receives the Holy Spirit as the indwelling presence of Almighty God the moment that person is born again. The Holy Spirit, the Third Person of the Trinity abides every day, in the heart of the born again one (see 1 Corinthians 3:16; 6:19-20).

- Every true born again believer should be – and can be – filled with the Holy Spirit. When the born again one is filled with the Spirit (Ephesians 5:18) he or she will **walk** by the Spirit, and will not fulfill the lusts of the flesh (see Romans 8:8-11; 12:1-2).

- The Holy Spirit helps every true believer in his or her prayer life:

"Likewise the Spirit also helps in our weaknesses. For we do not know what we should pray for as we ought, but the Spirit Himself makes intercession for us with groanings which cannot be uttered. Now He who searches the hearts knows what the mind of the Spirit is, because He makes intercession for the saints according to the will of God" (Romans 8:26-27).

The weakness spoken of here is not physical but is defined by the context, which speaks of prayer. The Holy Spirit helps in every way – but in the matter of prayer *He does in the heart what Christ does before God in heaven* (see v. 34). These verses should comfort even the weakest saint. Note again the promises:

- The Spirit helps us when we pray.
- The Spirit helps us when we are burdened and broken with grief and heartaches.
- The Spirit groans *within us* and God understands the groanings of the Spirit, even groanings which cannot be uttered – because the Spirit utters request according to the will of God.
- I'm sure that every child of God reading this section recall one time or another when you were so burdened you could not utter words of prayer. All you could say was "O Lord …. Help me …. Have mercy!" or similar words. But the Holy Spirit knows the burden, the desire, the longings of the believer's heart; therefore, He helps us in such an hour. Praise God!
- One day all these groanings will cease, and we will experience the glorious deliverance that is coming in the *"salvation ready to be revealed in the last time"* (1 Peter 1:5).

The Saints blessings in all things

Romans 8:28 is one of the most comforting and beloved verses in the Bible. Again, I remind, this precious verse is for those *in Christ* only. I stress this because of the popularity of *inclusivity*, which like so many terms has been redefined to include the secular humanists' satanic slant, leading some even in the Christian community to believe that the truths of God's Word are subject to this relative deception. The Scripture assures us,

"And we know that all things work together for good to those who love God, to those who are the called according to His purpose."

The verse opens with the assurance that: *"We know!"* But what is it that we know? We know that in His providence, God orchestrates every event in life – even suffering, temptation, and sin – not a few things, not the good things, not the glorious things, but ALL things *"work together for **good** to them that love God ......"* the whatever, or whenever – they ALL work together for our good and for the glory of God if we love Him! *"...... to them who are called according to His purpose;"* "His purpose" is the very center of this verse.

If salvation was offered to us on a condition, that is, if it was left to our faithfulness, obedience, prayerfulness, or our ability – then the case would be hopeless and out of the question. Throughout history human beings have proven to break down under probation. The Law was such a system. Under the Law, life was offered as a *condition of obedience* to the Law: For Moses writes about the righteousness which is of the law, *"The man who does those things shall live by them"* (Romans 10:5). But the Law proved to be a burden which man **alone** could not bear (see Acts 15:10). The Law was a ministration of condemnation and death (see II Corinthians 3:7-9).

In the gracious Gospel of the *grace of God,* all conditions were swept aside. The invitation of the Gospel is to "whosoever will" ..... 'whosoever shall call" ... "let him that is thirsty come;" the invitation is simply, *"Come."* Almighty God does the rest!

STUDY GUIDE: CHAPTER 7

1. Jesus said, "seek food which endures to _____."

2. Jesus said, "I am the _____ of life.

3. Many read the Word but try to run their lives in their _____.

4. We find the _____ of God only in Jesus Christ.

5. In the _____ Jesus is seen as God embodiment in a human body life.

6. Christianity is more than a religion it is a _____ .

7. Jesus is the only _____ to God and _____.

8. Nichodemus a _____ of the Jews didn't have a clear answer of who _____ was.

9. When sin came it _____ the _____ of God in which human beings were created.

10. Human beings are _____ meaning they are three in one: _____, _____, and _____ which is God's order.

11. The goal of _____ is to bring the whole person back in _____ _____ with God.

12. The Holy Spirit _____ the individual in regeneration.

13. We are reconciled to God through the _____ _____ of Christ.

14. Transformation for kingdom living and service begins with a
_____ .

15. Every true Christian has the _____ Holy
Spirit of God.

CHAPTER 8

COMMUNITY – THE NARROW WAY

The early Christians did not think that Christ had defeated the powers of evil in His living, dying, and resurrection without leaving a means by which this redeeming action would continue in the world. The church is seen as the sign of *Christus Victor,* the community of people where *the victory of Christ over evil becomes present in and to this world.* For this reason, the Apostle Paul spoke of the church as the community through which *"the manifold wisdom of God should be made known to the rulers and authorities in the heavenly realms."* (Ephesians 3:10)

Because it is impossible to give an exact definition of the church, the biblical writers always referred to the church through picture-images. It is reported that there are more than eighty images of the church in the New Testament. [For example salt and light, ark, etc.]. In his book, Ancient-Future Faith, Robert E. Webber, speaking from a study by Paul Minear reports that the four most dominant images of the church are: the people of God, the new creation, the fellowship in faith, and the body of Christ. These images speak to us of the theology of the church as *the presence of Christ in the world.* Webber concludes that this theological insight, that the church is the "community of God's presence" will have a far-reaching effect in the postmodern world, both for those who are within the church and for the unchurched.[35]

The People of God

The New Testament defines the church as "all the saints in Christ Jesus" (Philippians 1:1). The origin of the church then lies in the "finished redemptive work of Jesus Christ." Just as the origin of Israel is rooted in the exodus event so, the church is grounded in the Christ event – the primordial event of the Christian faith. For this reason the church is designated by words that compare it with Israel. The church is "a chosen race," "a holy nation," "the circumcision," "Abraham's sons," "heirs of David's throne," "a remnant," and "the elect."

The church, like Israel, is also viewed in terms of the future. The idea of the church moving toward a destination is common in the Bible (see Hebrew 12:2; Philippians 14:1). The church is a pilgrim people, an exiled people (Peter); a people who are at enmity with the world (James); a people who wrestle with diabolic powers (Paul), (Ephesians 6); and a bride (John), (Revelation 19:8).

The church is the most effective witness individually and corporately to a postmodern world of disconnected people. Postmodern people are not persuaded to faith by *reason* so much as they are moved to faith by participation in God's earthly community.[36]

The New Creation

The second image, "the new creation," speaks to the nature of God's earthly community. It is the community in which a new start in life begins. As Paul said in 2 Corinthians 5:17: *"Therefore, if anyone is in Christ, he [or she] is a new creation; the old has gone, and the new has come."* This new creation is to be taken in both an individual and a corporate sense – a new person, a new community of people. The Christian is the product of God's power to create, for only God can create a *new heart* and a *new spirit* in the bosom of the person who exercises faith in the shed blood of Jesus. When an addict, a liar, a thief, or a fornicator to name a few believes on Jesus and becomes a born again child of God, the drugs, alcohol, sex, pornography, lying or other sins *disappear* form his or her life. *Evil* proceeds from the heart and when God "new births" one into His family He creates in that person a new heart, a new life, and give that one of His divine nature.

Although the tares are raising their heads in the churches [sinful conduct and behavior] the saints must be steadfast in God's Word. New converts must be taught that: "...old things **pass** away; behold, **all** things become new." Paul is speaking of *old habits and practices of life, but he is also speaking of old views of Christ.* The "new creation" is the context in which our journey of faith is taking place. A born again believer's understanding *changes*. As a sinner he or she may say, "I cannot understand the Bible." When born again, however, that person recognizes that while he or she may not understand *all* of God's Word – they do understand many, many passages that were formerly closed to their unregenerate mind. Thus, as new believers study and walk in the light God sheds on their pathway through study of the Word, their understanding becomes clearer and clearer. The mind now changes about God. New thoughts about God take over. There are new thoughts concerning this world and the world to come. There are new views of biblical truth and duty to God. The Bible becomes a new Book. The church becomes a new place. Other Christians become new friends and there is a new beauty about everything. The believer sees the universe with new eyes of understanding because of their new heart. A new love for family and friends arises. New feelings rise in the heart toward all humanity. Verses 18 and 19:

Now all things are of God, who has reconciled us to Himself through Jesus Christ, and has given us the ministry of reconciliation, that is, that God was in Christ reconciling the world to Himself, not imputing their trespasses to them, and has committed to us the word of reconciliation.

God has made us a new creation *in Christ* and has given us the ministry of reconciliation meaning "a change of relation from enmity to peace." We who have been reconciled to God have *the privilege* of telling others that they can be reconciled to Him as well. Praise God! He can do this because instead of us, He imputed our sins to Christ – in other words, God placed our sins on Christ who knew no sin. This is good news that everybody needs to hear today! The fellowship of the community itself nurtures and forms our pilgrimage.

The Fellowship in Faith

This is why the church as a fellowship in faith emphasizes the *divine presence* taking form in a new fabric of human relationships – a fellowship of people. **This fellowship shares a corporate life of** *"one heart and one soul"* (Acts 4:32). The character of the "fellowship in faith" is to be far different from the character of other communities:

- "There is neither Jew nor Greek, there is neither slave nor free, there is neither male nor female" (Galatians 3:28).
- "For we do not preach ourselves, but Jesus Christ as Lord, and ourselves as your servants for Jesus' sake" (2 Corinthians 4:5).
- A servant to God immediately transforms relations on the horizontal level. No longer can one person "lord it" over another. All of God's people are equal before God and each other. For this reason the church is called the "family of God" (1 Peter 4:17).
- We all serve in God's house under God's authority. It is important to acknowledge that the church is a fellowship of faith, a corporate existence under God. A mutual servant hood to each other.

The church as the realized experience of the "fellowship of faith" will break down our *extreme individualism.* The Protestant Reformation had as its explicit purpose to return the church to a more biblical foundation. Some unintended side effects were:

- Splintering the church into multiple denominations.
- Telling believers that only the Scripture is the Christian's ultimate authority.
- That God's revelation is given today only through the Word.
- Emphasizing the priesthood of the individual believer (all biblically true).

The seeds were sown for individuals to stand ultimately **above** the church, judging it and **not** considering themselves accountable to it—*but rather the other way around!* In other words, rather than Scripture being one's final authority, one's *private interpretation of Scripture is!* This private interpretation has given rise not only to denominations splitting from one another on various points of theology to Para-church organizations that stand beyond the authority of the church, and believers who love Jesus but not the institutional church and are leaving in great numbers.

Revival based scriptural truth is needed:

- Through His finished work on the cross, Christ offers to sinners the chance to have an individual relationship with Him, not just with the church and its traditions as many were led to believe.

- It is true that salvation comes through repentance and a relationship with Christ, not through following church traditions.
- But once again, the unintended consequence was further *individualism* in church membership.
- Due to dissatisfaction with the church many families and individuals have begun experiencing other models of church concepts.

Consequently, the challenge of the church in the postmodern world is to recover community within the local church and the community of the entire church throughout history. We must learn that we are members of the *whole* church, the living and the dead, who constitute the fellowship of the faith.[37]

The Body of Christ

The image of the body proclaims that the people of God are a physical body of people who truly are the continuation of the presence of Christ in the world. In Romans 5:12-21, Paul explains, the "body of Christ" is understood as antithetical to the "body of death."

Here are the two humanities:

Those who stand in solidarity with Adam and constitute the "body of death."

- Those who stand in solidarity with Christ and constitute the "body of life."

This metaphor says that Christ is one with the church; the existence of the church is an essential continuation of the life of Jesus in the world. The church is a divine creation which, in a mystical yet real way, coexists with the Son who is made present through it.

The body image to the early church depicted the church as a new order, a new humanity, which has the power to be an explosive force in society and in history. It is called not to contain the message but to live its message, calling all people to repentance from the old into the new body!

These four images:

- The people of God
- The new creation
- The fellowship of faith
- The body of Christ

All four describes the connection that exists between the Christ victorious over sin and the Christ immediately present in the church. It is a new society that acts as "the sign of redemption" to the world. In the postmodern world the most effective churches will be those with a theological understanding and practice of the church as the community of God's presence in the world.[38]

The Glorious Community

Since the church is the community of God's presence in the world; we are a *special* people of purpose – God's purpose! And that purpose is to live the narrow way [from the worldview of the Scriptures] in fellowship with God, each other, and creation. If we would be the community our Lord desires us to be, we must gain a clear understanding of what community is. Only as we remind ourselves what we can be by the grace of God will we begin to draw on the great Power within our community – the Holy Spirit whom Christ has given to us. Under the guidance of the Holy Spirit we desire to live out in the present the glorious community for which God created us.

This glorious community is not a club we join; neither is it some large organization pandering for public opinion driven by ungodly cultural influence. Jesus said, *"No one can come to Me unless the Father who sent Me draws him; and I will raise him up in the last day"* (see John 6:44). Many individuals and ministries cave in to the culture and the world for various reasons; perhaps they were not drawn by the Father in the first place. Much of what is called worship today resembles that of a nightclub; the moves may be a little different, but the soul motives are the same. We are a people *in relationship* with the God who saves us through Christ and a people *in relationship* to each other – who *together* share in God's salvation. As a people in relationship with one another, we are a fellowshipping people, loyal to Christ – which defines who we are.

Fellowshipping was critical for the early disciples of Christ to function. Fellowshipping is also critical for us today. When the church stops being a fellowship, it becomes an organization. As an organization it may become known for its music, preaching, programs or some other special feature that makes it unique from the others, but if it does not have quality fellowship, it's just another social organization. God designed the church to be an organism; a live, pulsating, breathing, dynamic living fellowship.

There are many misconceptions of this concept of fellowship. The most common is to equate fellowship with a special activity. Sadly, with the church fellowship is normally linked to "food and fun." Christians especially are heard saying to each other, "Why don't you come over to my house for some food and fellowship?" We also associate fellowship with a place. "What do we call the place at church where we all gather for social activities and meals?" (We call it the fellowship hall). When reduced simply to a gathering or a place it is robbed of its true significance.

It takes quite a lot more than an event, a menu, or a program for authentic fellowship. The Greek word translated "fellowship" is *koinonia*. It means basically, "to have in common," a word for commonness to define our sharing together; our common participation, in the body of Christ.

The Apostle John gives us some insight on true fellowship in the opening verses of 1 John 1:1-4.

"What was from the beginning, what we have heard, what we have seen with our eyes, what we beheld and our hands handled, concerning the Word of Life – and the life manifested, and we have seen and bear witness and proclaim to you the eternal life, which was with the Father and was manifested to us – what we have seen and heard we proclaim to you also, that you also may have fellowship with us; and indeed our fellowship is with the Father, and with His Son Jesus Christ. And these things we write, so that our joy may be complete."

Individualism has entered a breech in the American churches' defenses and has successfully demolished the fellowship within many Christian communities. Today many people seem to try to sneak into the church and remain as quiet as possible without talking to anyone and carry themselves in a manner that screams, "Don't touch!" A great number of Christians find their greatest satisfaction or fulfillment *not with others,* but alone. The one-way conversation of the television becomes their best friend. It will talk to you without requiring you to talk back.

I experienced this first hand when one of our senior members was admitted to the hospital. I was visiting her when one of her grandchildren told her someone had broken into her home and stole the TV and some other items, but the idea of going home to no TV frightened her and she was really sick then. She told the doctor she couldn't go home. Of course her children replaced the TV and she went home.

In the Scripture above, John says there is a direct connection between the fullness of your fellowship and the extent of your joy as a child of God. Church members walk right pass one another and in some cases have never been formally introduced. Even in the so-called fellowship hall they all just pass each other with a nod; both fellowship and relationships are gone.

The point is clear! The church is more than a loosely related group of people. The New Testament writers referred to the church as a nation, a body, a new creation, and a fellowship of faith. Though these people transcend spatial and temporal boundaries, it is chiefly manifested in a visible congregation of believers who band together [church] to be the local manifestation of Christ in the world. When fellowship is lost – joy just gradually makes a hasty exist (gone). The completeness of your joy is dependent on the richness of your fellowship – therefore, if you are not experiencing dynamic fellowship, something is missing and your Christian life goes lacking.

A Future-Oriented People

Jesus prophesied two thousand years ago that the gates of hell shall not prevail against the church; and He will return for a church without spot or wrinkle. Civilizations and nations have risen and have fallen, but the church keeps marching on. Many people rely on the media for their definition of the things that are seen; that includes the local congregations of God's people in specific places.

Sadly the Hollywood stereotypes are all that many people have to go by. However, the church is Spirit-formed into a people through whom He can bring about the completion of God's work in the world. We participate in one body, a worldwide fellowship composed of all believers of all ages. In Hebrews 12:22-23, the writer says,

> *But you have come to Mount Zion*
> *and to the city of the living God,*
> *the heavenly Jerusalem,*
> *to the innumerable*
> *company of angels,*
> *to the general assembly*
> *and church of the firstborn*
> *who are registered in heaven,*
> *to God the Judge of all,*
> *to the spirits of just men made perfect.*

The church is by no means an end in itself. God has not called us out of the world to become a little clique here and a little clique there, a center of entertainment here and a social club there. Rather we are a future-oriented people and our task is geared toward a grand finale at the end of the age. The church emerged in the context of Jesus' announcement, *"The kingdom of God is near"* (Mark 1:15).

God's kingdom is a gracious gift God will bestow on us one day. However, with the arrival of the King a new era in God's dealing with humankind had come:

"But when the fullness of time had come God sent forth His Son, born of a woman born under the law" (Galatians 4:4).

God sent His son into the world at the precise moment to bring all who would *believe* out from under bondage of the law. Like all men, Jesus was obligated to obey God's law. He also had to be fully man so He could take upon Himself the penalty of sin as the substitute for man (see Luke 1:32, 35; John 1:1, 14, 18). Unlike anyone else, however, He perfectly obeyed that law (see John 8:46; 2 Corinthians 5:21; Hebrews 4:15; 7:26; 1 Peter 2:21; 1 John 3:5).

As stated in earlier sections, His sinlessness made Him the unblemished sacrifice for sin, who "fulfilled all righteousness," perfectly obeyed God in everything. That perfect righteousness is what is imputed to [the accounts] of those who believe on Him.

Since Pentecost the Holy Spirit's saving, guiding, teaching, and miracle-working Kingdom power has been at work in our world. All believers in Christ receive His indwelling presence giving them a new dimension of power for witnessing. In Ephesians 3:16-19) the Apostle Paul prays,

"That He would grant you, according to the riches of His glory, to be strengthened with might through His Spirit in the inner man, that Christ may dwell in your hearts through faith; that you, being rooted and grounded in love, may be able to comprehend with all saints what is the width and length and depth and height – to know the love of Christ which passes knowledge; that you may be filled with all the fullness of God."

"Now to Him who is able to do exceedingly abundantly above all that we ask or think, according to the power that works in us" (v. 20).

The apostles' mission of spreading the gospel was the major reason the Holy Spirit empowered them (see Acts 1:8). This event dramatically altered world history, and the gospel eventually reached all parts of the earth, the narrow way (see Mathew 28:19, 20).

Two Ways of life

Like the Garden of Eden event, the church event has suffered the same infiltration by Satan. Since Eden as prophesied there has been continuous enmity between God and Satan. So the Lord God said to the serpent,

*"Because you have done this, you are cursed more than all cattle, and more than every beast of the field; on your belly you shall go, and you shall eat dust all the days of your life. **And I will put enmity between you and the woman, and between <u>your seed</u> and <u>her Seed;</u> He shall bruise your head, and you shall bruise His heel"*** (Genesis 3:15).

This *"first gospel"* is prophetic of the struggle and its outcome between "your seed" (Satan and unbelievers who are called the *"children of the devil"* in John 8:44) and her seed *"Christ,* a descendant of Eve, and *"those in Him."* Who are called the *"children of God."* Christ will one day destroy Satan, the serpent. Satan could only "bruise" Christ's heel (cause Him to suffer), while Christ will bruise Satan's head (destroy him with a fatal blow). In a passage of Scripture very similar to Genesis 3, Paul encouraged the believers in Rome, *"And the God of peace will crush Satan under your feet shortly"* (Romans 16:20).

True Christians should recognize that they participate in the crushing of Satan because, along with Christ, their Savior and His *finished work on the cross,* they also are the woman's seed. Likewise, we are instrumental at keeping him at bay through the power of the Holy Spirit today during this age of the church. Jesus taught of this battle of the seeds in the parable of the wheat and tares.

The two seeds in the Bible

Genesis 3:15 (the first evangel verse) is the first mention of the two seeds in the Bible. Using the Bible-study aid of first mention; we know that these two seeds and their enmity will run throughout the entire stewardship of humanity, just as prophesied in Genesis 3; and as Christians we should remember the battle is the Lord's!

- When Cain murdered Abel (see Genesis 4:1-16) he started this *enmity* between the two seeds [the children of God and the children of the devil]. First John 3:12, states that Cain was *"of the wicked one"* – a child of the devil.
  We find similar activity continuing throughout the entire Old Testament. Even in the interim period Satan's seed, the Pharisees and Sadducees opposed John the Baptist (Matthew 3:7) and **did nothing** when he was killed by Herod.
- These same "children of the devil," the Pharisees opposed Christ (Matthew 12:34; 23:33) and **asked to have Him crucified.** At the cross, Satan bruised Christ's heel but Christ bruised Satan's head and defeated him forever!

Wherever Christ "plants" His true Christians [seed/ wheat] to bear fruit for His glory (see Acts 18:8) – Satan then plants his false Christians [seed/ tares] to oppose the work and hinder the harvest. The enmity between the seeds continues throughout the New Testament and the [church age].

In Acts 5:11 we find the *first use* of the word "church," although it is the most common word used to describe the assembly of those who had believed. True believers understood that all they had belonged to God and that when a brother or sister had a need those who meet it were obligated to do so. The early believers lived in a commune or pooled and redistributed everything equally. The method was to give the money to the apostles who would distribute it (vv. 35, 37). Notice some of the conflicts of the two seeds for example:

- Peter and John were opposed by Sadducees as they preached Jesus in the resurrection (Acts 3:11-26; 4:2-4; 5:22-33).
- We find two examples of hypocrisy in the church in Ananias and Sapphira who held back a portion of the money from the sale of a certain possession which they no doubt promised the Lord he would give. Asked about the money Ananias lied. Peter said, "Satan filled your heart to lie to the Holy Spirit." (see Acts 5:1-10) Their sins of selfishness, faking their spirituality to impress others, and as they were in the church with true believers (v. 4:32) and were involved with the Holy Spirit 9v. 3), but they remained hypocrites. As a result of the divine judgment of death on Anaias and Sapphira the people were afraid about the seriousness of hypocrisy and sin in the church. And "Great fear came upon the church ...." (v. 11). While unbelievers had great respect for the believers but stayed away due to fear of the consequence of sin. Multitudes of unbelievers heard the gospel, and gladly believed. Notice the response of the children of the devil. "..... And the Saducees were filled with indignation" (v. 17).

For Servants Only

Because of the tremendous growth of the church, which included the Hellenist Jews from the diaspora the apostles advised the church to select seven men **"full of the Holy Spirit"** to take over the task of serving the tables (see Acts 6:1-4) while they spent their time in prayer and the ministry of the Word (v. 4).

I think the church is handed a great disservice with the idea that the passage in Acts 6 refers to deacons only. Vine's Greek Dictionary states that the so-called seven deacons are not there mentioned by that name, though the kind of service in which they were engaged was **of the character** of that committed to such.[39] I believe that this not only refers to the seven but would be the same criteria for any other anointed and appointed person or persons selected for any position in the church work or work of the church, especially any position of leadership. So no matter what place of service any Christian is placed being "full of the Holy Spirit" has to be the first prerequisite. In my pastoring, I placed much emphasis on the necessity of the ministry of the Holy Spirit in all areas of church life. The Greek term *"Diakonos"* views "servant" in relationship to his or her duties. All Christians are to be Spirit-filled (Ephesians 5:18). I venture to say that these are the only people who can counter the devil's counterfeit plants in the local church. In Matthew 13, the parable of the sower illustrates the church and the Christians' ability to hear, receive and understand the truth of God's Word and with wisdom and availability determine their readiness for service. Certainly this can only be accomplished through believers who are Spirit-filled and empowered:

> *"You shall receive power after the Holy Spirit*
> *has come upon you"* (see Acts 1:8).

It is so sad that many churches do not believe that training is necessary because they assume the Holy Spirit will do the teaching, however, many times these same people will select people based on their secular qualifications over the Spiritual qualifications. Please keep this section in mind as you read the next section.

Three kinds of unfruitful soil (Matthew 13:3-9)

- Some receive seed [Word] by the wayside and Satan comes and snatches it away, because of shallow understanding of what they hear (v. 4). [*unfruitful*]
- Some receive seed [Word] on stony places, and though received with joy they don't have deep roots to endure when tribulation and persecution arises because of the word, immediately they stumble (v. 5-6). [*unfruitful*]
- Some receive the seed [Word] among thorns who hear the Word and the cares of the World and deceitfulness of riches choke the word and he or she becomes unfruitful (v. 7). [*unfruitful*]

Branches that do not bear fruit (vv. 2, 6). The unfruitful branches are those who profess to believe, but their lack of fruit indicates that they have never been genuinely saved and they have no life from the vine.

Three kinds of good fruitful soil (Matthew 13:8, 23)

Some receive the seed [Word] on the good soil is he or she who hears and understands it, who indeed bears fruit and produces some a hundredfold, some sixty, some thirty (v 23) [*fruitful*].

In John 15, using the metaphor of the vine and branches, Jesus clarifies the good soil [a pure heart]. He identifies Himself as the *"true vine"* and the Father as the *"vinedresser"* or caretaker of the vine: Fruitful branches that bear fruit (vv. 2, 8). The fruitful vines are planted in good soil. The branches that bear fruit are the true genuine Christians, the children of God down through the ages. Jesus said,

"By this My Father is glorified, that you bear much fruit; so you will be My disciples" (John 15:8). *"But he who received seed on the good soil is he who **hears the word and understands it,** and indeed bears fruit and produces:*

- *Some (good soil) a hundredfold*
- *Some(good soil) sixty,*
- *Some (good soil) thirty"* (Matthew 13:23).

As there were three kinds of soils **with no fruit,** thus no salvation – there are three kinds of good soils **with fruit.** Not all true Christians are equally fruitful, but all are fruitful. Jesus said, "You will know them by their fruit" (see Matthew 7:16).Branches that do not bear fruit (vv. 2, 6). The unfruitful branches are those who profess to believe, but their lack of fruit indicates that they have never been genuinely saved and they have no life from the vine.

The New Testament describes "fruit" as:

- Godly attributes (Galatians 5:22, 23; also review pages 55-58 in chapter 4).
- Righteous behavior (Philippians 1:11).
- Praise (Hebrews 13:15).

- Especially leading others to saving faith in Jesus Christ (see Romans 10:9-10; John 3:16).
- **The Narrow Way**
  In Matthew 7:13-14, two ways are offered to people. Both ways, the narrow and the wide way promises to provide the entrance to God's kingdom. As I pointed out in a prior section, the narrow way (gate) is by faith, only through the finished work Christ.

Nor is there salvation in any other, for there is no other name under heaven given among men by which we must be saved" (Acts 4:12).

It represents genuine salvation in God's way that leads to eternal life. The wide gate *includes all religions of works and self-righteousness* that claims all ways lead to God.

STUDY GUIDE: CHAPTER 8

1. The four most dominant church images are the:
   _____
   _____.

2. The _____ is the most _____ weapon to a postmodern world.

3. The new creation is to be taken in both _____ and _____ sense.

4. The church as the "fellowship of faith" will break down our _____.

5. Rather than the Scripture being the final authority one's _____ of Scripture is.

6. The existence of the church is an _____ _____ of the life of Jesus in the world.

7. God's purpose is that we live the narrow way in _____ with God, each _____ and _____.

8. As a people in relationship with one another, we are a _____, loyal to Christ which _____ who we are.

9. The Greek word translated fellowship is _____.

10. There is a direction connection between _____ and the extent of your _____.

11. Jesus prophesied two thousand years ago that the _____ _____ shall not prevail against the church.

12. All believers in Christ receive His _____ _____ giving them a new dimension of power.

13. First gather the _____ and bind them in bundles to burn them, but gather _____ into my barn.

14. Then the _____ will shine forth as the _____ in the kingdom of their Father.

15. There are 3 types of bad soil and three types of good soil. List each below.
    1.
    2.
    3.
    4.
    5.
    6.

CHAPTER 9

GUIDANCE – THE NARROW WAY

There are those who say that God cannot and will not guide us today. Others will simply tell you, "God led me ….." Life in today's world seems a confused mess with its moral pollution, physical and sexual abuse, empty political promises, wars, uncontrolled abuses, unemployment, tight economy, and a society who thinks the most you can do is make the best of it. This attitude is running rampart in some Christian communities.

Or is there a right way? The Greeks had a word *hamartia* to describe this way and it meant "to miss the mark." All of our strivings to find ourselves is with a single purpose in mind. We don't want to miss the mark. Yet most people and some of them in the church miss the mark because they really don't know what the mark is. This utter confusion among us stems from the fact that *they believe all wisdom comes from the same source,* [human beings].

The Bible teaches very clearly that this is not true. There is wisdom from above: **[from God]**. And there is wisdom from below: **[from Satan]**. Both wisdoms are from supernatural sources. Both are sought after. Both can be **found**. Additionally the Bible teaches that:

- The wisdom from above is *truth* – "right" and leads us to hit the target.
- The wisdom from below is *false* – "wrong" and causes us to miss the target.

The Scripture teaches that it is possible to distinguish one from the other. The proof of the pudding is always in the eating. There are obvious and predictable results from following either one.

The Greek word *"hamartia,"* to miss the mark is translated in our English Bible as *"sin."* The Bible teaches that we are all born sinners – unable to hit the mark on our own. But the Bible also teaches that God has made necessary provisions for our condition. He sent Jesus Christ, His only begotten Son, to die on the cross for our missing the mark [sin], thereby reconciling us to a right relationship with God, our Father. God made the provision:

- But each of us must accept it for him or herself.
- Each of us is given the freedom of choice.
- Our individual destiny is determined by what we choose.
- We can accept or reject our relationship with God in Christ.

The Word of God tells us:

- That Jesus is the way, the truth, and the life and that *no one can come to the Father any other way!*
- That salvation is the unmerited gift of God, not something we have earned by our works of goodness.
- That we are not saved by our own wisdom, cleverness, or works, but by faith in the finished work of Jesus Christ.
- That it is totally impossible for us to know what life is all about until we take that first step – toward the purposes of God in our own lives.
- That Jesus declared that He knew from where He came, who He was, and where He was going (John 8:14).
- That He desires to bring the same to each of us; that we may be one.

The Secret of Christianity

The Apostle Paul tells us that the secret to Christianity is that Christ actually dwells **in** the believer and *guides them by faith*. God has made several provisions for our guidance:

(1) Jesus Christ in us,

(2) The baptism in the Holy Spirit, and

(3) The Word of God.

Therefore Christ *in us* is our hope of glory:

- With Jesus Christ in us we can focus in on what life is all about for us personally and corporately as His body [the Church].
- John the Baptist said, "those who repent of their sins and turn from them; Jesus would baptize them in the Holy Spirit."
- The Apostle Peter told the people on the Day of Pentecost: "Repent, and be baptized, *every one of you* in the name of Jesus Christ for the remission of sins, and you shall receive the gift of the Holy Spirit" [the Church was born] (see Acts 2:38).
- Jesus talked about what the Holy Spirit would do in the believer: "When He, the Spirit of truth, is come, He will guide you into all truth for He shall not speak of Himself, but whatsoever He shall hear, that shall He speak, and He will show you things to come" (John 16:13).
- God has made available for our guidance His Word, the Bible. Without the Word of God it is *impossible* to hit the mark.
- It is *impossible* for us to know the will and purposes of God; these must be *revealed* to us through the Holy Spirit and the truth of God's Word.
- Jesus told the Jews who believed on Him: *"If you continue in My word, then are you My disciples indeed; And you shall know the truth, and the truth shall set you free"* (John 8:31-32).

Once again we are faced with a choice; to accept the Word of God as truth or not. Our choice will determine our destiny, whether or not we'll hit the mark and move on into God's will and purposes for our lives. Everyone lives by some authority. Blessed is the person who makes God's Word to be his or her authority, Jesus said that if we do, we will never be put to shame.

I assume you have taken the first steps outlined in the Word of God: You've confessed and repented of your sins, accepted the finished work of Jesus Christ on the cross in your stead, and received the promise of the

Baptism in the Holy Spirit. Study, meditate and receive the revealed truth of God's Word.

Now that you have zeroed in on the wisdom from above – we understand that much of the confusion about guidance among Christians comes from the spiritual ignorance of not recognizing Satan's "counterfeit wisdom." He deals with both believers and non-believers, but he deals with each differently.

The Word of God promises that as a child of God you *can know* the perfect will of God for your life (see Romans 12:1-2); and know the joy, reality, and fullness of divine guidance. I don't want to overemphasize the danger of negative or false guidance, through Satan's counterfeit [religious Christianity]. However, it is important to sound a warning at the beginning in order to determine what guidance **is not!** Let me say at the outset:

---

*The truth of God's Word is the **only** antidote to lies and deceptions.*

Apart from His revelation, God forbids any attempts to know the future or to seek favor from any supposed to be God. In Deuteronomy 18, Moses warned Israel against following the pagans' occult practices of offering up a son or daughter to their idols for guidance that they might know the future – additionally the list of abominations Israel used to try to circumvent God's revelation includes the practice of witchcraft, or a soothsayer, one who interprets omens, or a sorcerer, or one who conjures up spells, or a medium, or a spiritist or one who calls up the dead (see vv. 10-12).

God then promised to send prophets to His people, like Moses, by whom God will give special guidance when it is needed. Further, Deuteronomy 18 gives three tests for distinguishing a true prophet from a false prophet.

The true prophet will:

1. Be "from among their brethren
2. Speak in God's name, and
3. Predict the future accurately." (v. 22)

In Deuteronomy 18, God makes it very clear that those who
know God are to have nothing to do with occult practices.

In Deuteronomy God emphasizes through Moses a truth that hold
true for us today. The fact was that God was motivated by love to give the
Israelites His Law, *and that only love for God can motivate a believer to obey
the Lord.*

Today many people use Satan's counterfeits as a means of guidance
to unveil hidden knowledge, ascertain future events, uncover secret
wisdom and exercise supernatural power. However, all of this and much
more can be found through the Holy Spirit. God's people [the Christian
community] must be willing to be delivered from this counterfeit form of
guidance in order to be genuine and biblical!

It is imperative for us to study and meditate on the
truth of God's Word in our hearts individually and
corporately – then through the ministry of the Holy
Spirit we can withstand every fiery dart of Satan!

It is so tragic that many misled uninformed people complicate Divine
guidance by the trickery of their own:

- legalism
- mixed-up emotions
- impure motives
- prejudices
- and old habit patterns of thought and action

It's at this time that many people commit terrible acts of horror and
immorality, and have heard *a voice,* but had they known God as He
reveals Himself through *His Word, His Spirit,* and *His Son,* they never
would have believed the false guidance and acted on it. It's also at this
point that some turn their backs [sometimes whole churches] in fear of a
deeper commitment to God's narrow way.

The importance of *having* the truth in you!

It is sad that in the midst of the crisis in the American Church, we have a conflict between the brethren. The conflict seems to be centered on whether or not the Holy Spirit's ministry is active in the church today. The question is has His ministry ceased in the church since His work on the Day of Pentecost? Many are saying that God has spoken through His Son in the Scriptures and that's that. Then on the other hand there are those who testify of deep experiences in the realm of the Spirit and look down on those brethren that are not there yet.

I heard a brother exclaim one day, "If we could take the experience of the Pentecostal and put it in a person along with the doctrinal knowledge of the Baptist – the results would be one true saint." I believe we must have a balance of both in every child of God. The way I see it, the early church had that balance as long as they stuck with the apostles' doctrine, prayer and the breaking of bread.

After the Apostle Paul was martyred the persecuted church went underground – the church that emerged set aside much of the truth of God's Word for its own doctrine *[putting human interpretation over God's revelation]*. The true church has been in the minority [in numbers] ever since. The results of this drastic change over the centuries in the churches' doctrines, traditions and customs have overshadowed the biblical doctrinal truths of the Bible throwing much of the church into an apostate condition and in need of deliverance. Those churches that have sought deliverance through renewal and have gotten their biblical worldview and doctrine back into proper perspective and practice understand what Paul meant:

"There is therefore now no condemnation to those who are in Christ Jesus, who do not walk according to the flesh, but according to the Spirit" (Romans 8:1).

In contrast with the preceding description of sinfulness in Romans 7:25, the Apostle Paul depicts the freedom of *living* in the Spirit. There is no condemnation in Christ, we are no longer under the sentence of the law, but the Church is *empowered* by the Holy Spirit to live in Christ. To walk in the Spirit means to obey the prompting and leading of the Holy Spirit. A believer or church following the Spirit's lead will not become conceited and provoke others or envy others (v. 16). Here lies the fallacy of walking in the flesh as so many prefer to do and think:

"Because what may be known of God is manifest in them, for God has shown it to them. For since the **creation** *of the world His invisible attributes are clearly seen, being understood by the things that are made, even His eternal power and Godhead, so that they are without excuse"* (Romans 1:19-20).

The **truth** that human beings *purposely ignore or suppress* is the fact that a Creator God exists. Satan, through secular humanism and multiculturalism is gaining ground daily with the suppression of truth in all of our institutions, media and especially public opinion. In his book, the Smart Guide to the Bible, Dr. Larry Richards compares Paul's point in the creation to a great radio transmitter, broadcasting the message of His existence. The Greek uses a different phrase in the clause; *God has made it plain to them.* The Greek says in that God has made it plain *"in them."* He continues, "God not only shaped the universe to send the message that He formed all that exists; God also shaped human nature with a built-in receiver, tuned to God's station."

Human beings who *suppress* or *purposely ignore* **the truth** of God's existence are without excuse, because to **reject** or **ignore God** they must have willfully "turned down" their inner receiver. *Human beings have willfully refused to accept the message God is broadcasting.*[40]

"Because, although they knew God, they did not glorify Him as God, nor were thankful, but became futile in their thoughts, and their foolish hearts were darkened" (Romans 1:21).

The proper response to God's revelation of Himself in creation is to give Him praise for His mighty works and give Him thanks. Rather than do this, humans have suppressed **the truth that God exists and deserves our worship.**

"Therefore God also gave them up to uncleanness, in the lusts of their hearts, to dishonor, their bodies among themselves, who exchanged **the truth of God for the lie,** *and worshipped and served the creature rather than the Creator, who is blessed forever, Amen"* (Romans 1:24-25).

The phrase "gave them up" is repeated in Romans 1:26, and "gave them over" in 1:28. The sexual impurity and other sins he describes in this chapter are clear evidence that God's wrath is directed **against those who reject Him** (see v. 28). Our American culture grows more morally corrupt with each passing day, just as those who committed such sin in their bodies in the passage with the same promised results (see Romans 1:18). God created humankind in His own image, with the capacity to love, and respond to love.

When human beings abandon God and suppress the truth about Him – he or she has openly welcomed to themselves all that is evil! The very existence of such evil as we experience daily in our society is evidence *of humankind's abandonment of God*. Sin may look attractive, especially when we first enter into it, but sooner than later it will make you miserable in the absence of the joy and peace of God.

*Who, knowing the **righteous judgment** of God, that those who practice such things are deserving of death, not only do the same but also approve of those who practice them* (Romans 1:32).

We witness to what Paul is saying here as we observe the people who defend immoral behavior that everyone knows to be so. Yet, these individuals and even some whole churches argue for privacy rights and the freedom to do what we wish without being subject to the morality police! Rather than taking a stand for what is right [the narrow way] such persons insist that others have the "right" to do what is wrong. The sins of flesh require the abandonment of God in trying to explain it.

Paul's point is that everyone, even those ignorant of God's revealed standards, still recognizes that:

* *Some things are morally right and*
* *Others are morally wrong.*

Societies not having access to God's standards – create their own standards. The point is every human being is born with a moral compass, so all of us are evaluating actions and behaviors to determine whether they are right or wrong. Even those persons who do not know the Law will be judged by their own moral standards. Though the Law cannot save us – through the Law we become conscious of sin:

- The Law was never intended as a standard we are to live up to.
- The Law was intended to be a mirror to show us how far short we are from what we ought to be.
- God's Word says there is no one righteous, not even one.

The roots of sin are anchored in mankind's rejection of God.

God's Solution (Reconciliation)

Jesus Christ died to pay the penalty for man's sin that through faith in Him those who believe might not only be forgiven but reestablish a personal relationship with God. And just as man's rejection of God produced sins in individuals and society, the restoration of a personal relationship with God will produce righteousness in those who are joined to Jesus Christ.

God by His own will used His Son, the only acceptable and perfect sacrifice as the means to reconcile unsaved individuals to Himself. God initiates the change; and He declares those who believe in Jesus to be righteous in His sight. The righteousness that God credits to the Christians account is the righteousness of Jesus Christ, God's Son.

Just as, Christ was not a sinner but was treated as if He was a sinner while taking our sins in His body on the cross – so true Christians who have been made righteous as the Father wrapped us in the righteousness of His dear Son are treated as if we are righteous or justified in the Son, a divine exchange! Praise God! God works in the believer's life to produce a righteousness that we could never manifest apart from Him (see 2 Corinthians 5:21).

Ambassadors for Christ

*"Now then, we are ambassadors for Christ, **as though God were pleading through us,** we implore you on Christ's behalf, be reconciled to God"* (2 Corinthians 5:20).

As Christ's representatives in the world, like Paul, we are responsible for bearing His message to the unsaved. His message is one of peace:

- God has paid the price for your sin.
- God is not at war with sinners.
- Sinners can now believe and be saved.

In his *Expository Outlines on the New Testament,* Dr. Warren Wiersbe would have us to consider:[41]

1. Ambassadors are **chosen**, and Christ had chosen Paul to be His representative. Paul did not represent himself, but Christ (see 2 Corinthians 4:5). His message was *the Gospel Christ had committed to his trust* (see 1 Thessalonians 2:4). His aim was to please Christ and be faithful to the task given to Him.
2. Ambassadors are **protected.** An ambassador must be a citizen of the nation that he or she represents, and Paul (as is every Christian) was a citizen of heaven (see Philippians 3:20) where "conversation" is equated with "citizenship." The nation supplies their ambassadors' every need and stood with him in every crisis.
3. Ambassadors are **held accountable.** Ambassadors represent their countries and say what they are instructed to say. They know that they must one day give an account of their work.
4. Ambassadors are **called home** before war is declared. God has not yet declared war on this wicked world, but one day He will. There is a coming day of wrath (1 Thessalonians 1:10) that will judge the wicked, but Christians will be called home before that day comes (1 Thessalonians 5:1-10). The church, God's ambassadors, will not go through the Tribulation.

The Scriptures reveal that the message of the church today remains one of reconciliation: God in Christ on the cross has reconciled the world to Himself and is willing to save all who will trust His Son. Wiersbe stresses that our message is not of social reform (although the Gospel reforms lives, Titus 2:11-15); ours is a message of spiritual regeneration. We represent Christ as we invite the lost to receive Him. What a responsibility!

All believers are ambassadors, whether we accept the commission or not. *"As the Father has sent Me, also I send you,"* said Christ (John 20:21). Let us make sure that our message, methods, and motives are right, so that our work might be lasting and might stand the test of fire when we stand before Him.

Like Paul, all true Christians who engage in a faithful ministry of reconciliation should expect to be rejected and accepted, to be hated and loved, to encounter joy and hardship. This is what Jesus had already taught His disciples (see Matthew 5:10-16; Luke 12:2-12).

"In all things we commend ourselves as ministers" (2 Corinthians 6:4). Paul lists the important elements of the righteousness God had granted him in vv. 6-7:[42]

- By the Holy Spirit – Paul lived and walked by the power of the Spirit (v. 6; see Galatians 5:16).
- By the Word of truth – During his entire ministry, Paul never operated beyond the boundaries of the direction and guidance of divine revelation (v. 7; see Colossians 1:5; James 1:18).
- By the power of God – Paul did not rely on his own strength when he ministered (v. 7; see 1 Corinthians 1:18; 2:1-2; Romans 1:16).
- By the armor of righteousness on the right and the left – Paul did not fight Satan with human resources but with spiritual resources (v.7; see Ephesians 6:10-16).

STUDY GUIDE: CHAPTER 9

1. The Greek word *"hamartia"* means to _____ _____.

2. According to Paul the secret to Christianity is _____.

3. Jesus said, "If you continue in My Word, then are you _____.

4. The _____ promises that the child of God can know the _____.

5. The true prophet is distinguished from the false prophet because:
    a. _____
    b. _____
    c. _____

6. Divine guidance is hindered in many Christians through _____ _____.

7. The true church is in the _____.

8. Reading through page 88 of the text; what is the great sin we must avoid _____?

9. Why did God "give them up?" Explain below:

10. The Law cannot _____ us, but through the Law we can become _____.

11. Christ died to pay the _____ for our sins.

12. God declares those who believe in Jesus to be _____.

13. It is impossible for us to know the will and purpose of God – except they be _____ to us by the Holy Spirit and the Word of God.

14. God has made His _____ available for our guidance.

15. God has made several provisions for our guidance – list them below:

    a.
    b.
    c.

CHAPTER 10

GODLINESS – THE NARROW WAY

Discipline in godliness is profitable in all things and affects both the present and future life of the believer. The present aspect includes obedience and a life on purpose (see John 10:10). The future aspect involves greater rewards at the coming of our Lord. We strive to please the Lord not only because we know we will be with Him, but because He will evaluate our work whether good or bad and reward us accordingly.

Be an example to other believers

In 1 Timothy 4:12, Paul admonishes young Timothy to be an example to other Christians. He had to live a mature life, a life that would be an example to other believers; that he be an example in word, in behavior, in love, in spirit, in faith, and purity. His counsel to be a mature example of faith is especially applicable to believers in this day marked by a culture of individualism and relativism:

- We are to be an example in word – not only in what we say, but how we say it.
- We have to allow the Spirit to control our conversation and tongue at all times.
- We are to be an example in behavior – Our conduct is to be disciplined and Spirit-controlled.
- We are to be an example in love – the kind the Christian is to have for all people is agape love, the great love of God Himself.

- We are to be an example in spirit – to walk led by the Spirit and keeping our minds upon spiritual things [spiritual-mindedness].
- We are to be an example in faith – that is, in faithfulness. We are to be loyal to the Lord Jesus and the church regardless of the demands, hardships, temptation, trials, or opposition.
- We are to be an example in purity – to live a moral, clean, just, and honest life. Completely free of coveting, lusting, worldliness, self-seeking, immorality, and all other known sins.

"Blessed are the pure in heart: for they shall see God" (Matthew 5:8).

We are to live a life of purity that far exceeds the standards of the world. Our lives are to be pure-perfectly pure! I'm sure that some of you reading this book are asking, "How am I going to live this life?" Take heart, at the center of all our experience is the life-giving power for effective life and service. I am referring to the personal presence and ministry of the Holy Spirit of God in us. There are those who believe and teach that the Spirit came on the Day of Pentecost and returned to heaven after the event. This group relies on science, reason in their natural senses striving to no avail to attain the example Paul spoke of above. The Scripture says,

*"The love of God has been shed abroad in our hearts through the **Holy Spirit** which was **given** unto us"* (Romans 5:5).

*"If any man [or woman] **does not have** the Spirit of Christ, he [or she] is none of His."* (Romans 8:9) Brackets mine.

God does not arbitrarily give His gifts at random, but they are given for a definite purpose to those who are His. God has truly, blessed us with every spiritual blessing in the heavenly places in Christ" (Ephesians 1:3). If those blessings which are ours in Christ are to become ours in experience, it is essential that we know the grounds on which we appropriate them. Peter admonishes,

"This Jesus God has raised up, of which we are all witnesses. Therefore being exalted to the right hand of God, and having received from the Father the promise of the Holy Spirit, He poured out this which you now see and hear. For David did not ascend into the heavens, but he says himself: The Lord said to my Lord, Sit at My right hand, till I make Your enemies Your footstools. Therefore let all the house of Israel know assuredly that God has made this Jesus, whom you crucified, Both Lord and Christ" (Acts 2:32-36).

In this section, let's consider verses 33 and 36 together:

- In verse 33 Peter states that the Lord Jesus was exalted *"at the right hand of God."* What was the result?
- He *"received of the Father the promise of the Holy Spirit."* And what followed? *"He poured out this which"* you now see and hear." Pentecost!

So, it was upon the fact of Jesus' exaltation to heaven that the Holy Spirit was given to the Lord Jesus to be poured out upon His people. The passage makes it very clear that the Holy Spirit was poured out because Jesus was exalted. The outpouring of the Spirit has no relation to your merits or mine, but only to the merits of our Lord and Savior, Jesus Christ. Notice, what we are does not come up, but only what He is. He is glorified; therefore the Spirit is poured out! Listen:

- Because the Lord Jesus died on the cross – I have received forgiveness of sins.
- Because the Lord Jesus rose from the dead – I have received new life.
- Because the Lord Jesus has been exalted to the right hand of the Father – I have received the outpoured Spirit.

All of this is because of Him; nothing is because of me.

- Remission of sins is not based on human merit – but on the Lord's crucifixion.
- Regeneration is not based on human merit – but on the Lord's resurrection.

- The baptism of the Holy Spirit is not based on human merit – but on the Lord's exaltation.

There are those who try to glamourize the baptism of the Holy Spirit. That person does not realize that the Holy Spirit was not poured out to prove how great we are or think we are, but to prove the greatness of the Son of God.

Peter has just referred to the outpouring of the Holy Spirit upon the disciples "which you see and hear." And he says, "Let the house of Israel therefore know assuredly that God has made both Lord and Christ, this Jesus whom you crucified." In essence, he said, "This outpouring of the Spirit, which you have witnessed with your own eyes and ears, proves that Jesus of Nazareth whom you crucified is now Lord and Christ." The Holy Spirit was poured out on earth to prove what has taken place in heaven – the exaltation of Jesus of Nazareth to the right hand of God. The purpose of Pentecost is to prove the Lordship of Jesus Christ.

It is sad that people are willing to fall for the ploy that the baptism of the Holy Spirit is only for a faithful few. This gift of the Holy Spirit is not given on the grounds of who we are or what we have done – but solely upon Christ and who He is and what He has done! It is all about Him. While all good and perfect gifts come down freely-given by the Father; however, for some there are conditions to be met on our part before we can receive them. In Acts 2:38-39, Peter said,

*"**Repent**, and let every one of you be **baptized** in the name of Jesus Christ for the **remission** of sins; and you shall receive the gift of the **Holy Spirit**. For the promise is to you and to your children, and to all who are afar off, as many as the Lord our God will call."*

I have put emphasis on four words in the text forming the conditions: Repent, baptism [are conditions] remission and the Holy Spirit [are gifts].

- Repent – refers to a change of mind or thinking and purpose that turns an individual from sin to God. Genuine repentance knows that sin must be forsaken and the person and work of our Lord and Savior, Jesus Christ embraced. Peter wants all to know that there is no conversion – unless the condition of repentance [a changed mind] is met.

- Baptism – baptism means "be immersed" in water. Peter was obeying the Lord's command from Matthew 28:19 and urging the people who repented and turned to the Lord Jesus Christ for salvation thus, to identify through water baptism with the death, burial, and resurrection of Jesus Christ (see Romans 6:3,4; 1 Corinthians 12:13; Galatians 3:27).

- Remission – Genuine repentance brings from God the forgiveness [remission] of sins (see Ephesians 1:7). New believers were to be baptized. Baptism, however, was to be the ever present act of obedience (Study Matthew 26:28; Colossians 2:13; 1 John 2:12).

- The Holy Spirit – Jesus repeatedly promised that God would send them His Spirit (see Luke 11:13; 24:49; John 7:39). The apostles had to wait until the Day of Pentecost, but since then all believers are baptized with the Holy Spirit at salvation (Study 1 Corinthians 12:13; Romans 8:9; 1 Corinthians 6:19-20). The promise of the gift was for all He calls.

God's Word of Counsel

There is a growing crowd of people attending church each Sunday, who live in despair, self-pity or holding a grudge against God because they have not heard from Him. They have found that most of what they receive is simply opinions or wild guesses.

A basic principle in the study of electricity when there is a problem always go first and check the source of power. If the headlights won't come on and you ask a friend, they might suggest that you replace the headlight assemblies. You do that and find that the headlights still don't come on. Another person suggests that you replace the headlight switch, so you replace the switch, but still no lights.

Finally, you grab that little owner's manual in the glove compartment. Open it to the table of contents and follow instructions to the troubleshooting section: Headlights fail to come on – check the battery. If the battery is fully charged – check the connection between the battery and the switch. You notice a little wire hanging down – then you see the terminal [from whence it came] connect the wire and bingo! The headlights come on. You remove the new headlight assemblies and switch – put the old parts back on. Then you find the receipt and head to the auto parts store for a refund. The parts clerk points to the fine print on the sales receipt: *No refund on electrical parts once they have been installed!*

A question we must *train* ourselves to ask when trying to seek the correct response to any problem or issue that arises is, *"What does God's Word say about this?"* In my years in ministry I have observed [one unchanging truth] – there is a vast difference between people who actually use God's Word in life's decisions, and those who simply go on instinct – or as the individual with the headlight problem above, operate on wild guesses or opinions of friends.

God did not create His world and then go off and leave it to defend itself. As King David said from personal experience in Psalm 23:1, *"The Lord is my Shepherd!"* He is in us and guides us on a path already prepared for us. As Christians, we do not worship a book; we worship the risen Christ. Yet the trustworthy witness to this Living Word of Christ is the Written Word of God.

Our Infallible Guide

The Bible is our infallible guide. In conjunction with the Spirit to direct our life, it's impossible to be led down the wrong path. We alone determine whether we want a large capacity by which God can guide us throughout our life – or a limited capacity. Allow the Holy Spirit to pour a lot of biblical revelation truth into your life, and He can speak into different areas of your life. However, give the Spirit only a few limited verses and *you limit* how far He can lead you.

There are times when God's written Word is very clear in helping us make specific decisions, for instance faithfulness, generosity, caring for the poor, and being the salt and *light. However, there are also times when the Scriptures don't seem to address a specific* problem or situation. In his book, "What's your Spiritual Quotient," Dr. Mark Brewer suggests three guidelines to help us understand the Scriptures in our decision-making processes:

1. *Knowing what God said and why He said it*
    The more we know what God has said, the more we can know what He is saying. Brewer's *first rule,* when we come to a particular passage is to ascertain what it meant to the "first

hearers." All verses have context in that they had specific reference and meaning when they were first written.

The more you and I ask, "What did it mean when it was first spoken?" the more we can know what God is saying to us today. Knowing about the times, the settings, the culture, and even the language of the first hearers of God's Word gives us more ability in applying the same truths to us today.[43]

2. *Interpretation and application*
While there is only one accurate interpretation of a passage, there can be many applications of the same passage. A particular verse, in its original setting and time, can be accurately interpreted only one way. However, the Holy Spirit may apply the interpretation in different ways for different situations.

That's why it's important that we don't skip over tough passages, but that we attempt to interpret them in light of the whole counsel of God This is because the Lord will often reveal something new to us by a verse we've read a hundred times before. The written Word is alive and active because of the fact that the living Word (the risen Christ) is alive to apply it to us.[44]

3. *Open your Heart*
We get out of the Bible what we bring to it. One of the greatest gifts the Holy Spirit gives in rightly discerning the Scriptures is that of removing pride. Very often our problem is not that the Bible may appear to contradict itself, but that it contradicts us – what we want it to say to support what we want to do.

It takes the hard work of study to release the Bible's wisdom. Lots of people have a little Bible from here and there, but are unwilling to really open up the Bible and study it --- to let it *teach* them![45]

I read a true story of a missionary's tour of some islands in the Pacific Ocean. He taught some Bible classes on the main island before moving on. He returned to the island a couple of years later and found all of the adults on the island born again Christians. They found a page of John's gospel which undoubtedly fell out of the old worn Bible carried by the missionary. God's Word is powerful! An island was transformed by a few passages of Scripture leading the right person who was prepared to listen and heed – in the right time. The more we know of God's written Word, the more we can be led by His living Word, Jesus Christ.

STUDY GUIDE: CHAPTER 10

1. Discipline in _____ is profitable in all things.

2. Paul admonishes Timothy to be an example in: _____, _____, _____, _____, _____, and _____.

3. We are to be loyal to the _____ and the _____ regardless of trials.

4. If a person does not _____ He or she is not a child of God.

5. The outpouring of the Spirit has no _____ to your _____ or _____.

6. The Holy Spirit was poured out because Jesus _____ _____.

7. List the two conditions required to receive the baptism of the Holy Spirit _____ and _____.

8. Genuine repentance brings _____ from God.

9. _____ were to be baptized.

10. Baptism was to be the ever present act of _____.

11. Jesus repeatedly promised that God would send the _____.

12. Jesus told the apostles to _____ for the _____.

13. The outpouring of the Holy Spirit has nothing to do with your merit or mine, but on Jesus Christ who is _____ to the right hand of God.

14. _____ is not based on human merit, but on the resurrection of our Lord and Savior, Jesus Christ.

15. The purpose of Pentecost is to prove the _____ _____ of Christ.

SECTION IV
RETHINKING CHURCH

CHAPTER 11

RE-THINKING CHURCH

A major concern facing the churches today is found in their methodology of how they "do church," as reflected in a particular church model. A visit to many of our traditional and institutional churches is like stepping into a time machine and going back in time seventy to one hundred years. While almost all other institutions and organizations are striving for relevance with the times – these traditional churches are locked into yester-year! So many people in our churches think, "It was good for my dear mother or father, or grand, so it's good enough for me." Someone quipped, the seven last words of a dying church are, "We have never done it like that!"

Changing how we do church to remain relevant is difficult. For many the church is the only place left you can go and expect it to be the same year after year. However, the gospel demands that we *re-think* our churches in considering others as well as ourselves. A case in point is our youth who are tomorrow's church. To put in bluntly, no youth – no church! Some time ago George Barna warned:

Faith is just one component in people's lives that helps them to interpret and cope with reality – and it certainly is not the central shaping influence for most people. The data regarding young adults also pose the possibility that churches are losing ground in terms of influence and may need to consider new approaches to making ancient truths more vivid and comprehensible in a technology-drenched, relativistic global community[46].

The question that every church faces as we assess what can or must change – likewise, what must never change?

Why are Churches Changing?

Some people are praying and working for churches to change and some are changing, but not all necessarily for the better. It has been said, if the typical church were to go to a hospital's emergency room, the physician would immediately admit it to the hospital and put it on life support. Churches are struggling all across America. Some have plateaued and are declining, while others are in the final stage of dying.

Often we Americans find it very hard to accept the blame for our mistakes. So we pass the buck. As I travel around this great nation the serious concern that confronts many traditional and institutional churches is declining congregations while at the same time the number of unchurched people including some Christians and non-Christian groups are growing. In 1998, a Barna report stated that there were 20 million unchurched Christians in America. His recent research has shown that that figure has increased to 117 million. That figure reflects the loss over the past 16 years, think about that!

Other Barna research revealed that 6% of people who have ever been to church say they learned something about God the last time they attended. The majority of people 61% say they did not gain any significant or new insights regarding faith when they last attended.[47]

Often the temptation is to look quickly for a solution, since the souls of people are at stake. However, we should realize that it took a while to reach that decline so we must thoroughly explore some of the reasons for it. Many times discovering the reasons for our problems lead to finding solutions to those problems and, in this case, may help to guide the development of future church models as well as discern good and bad present church models.

Why are Americans leaving the Church?

There was a time when you were expected to join the family church and remain there for life. However, that no longer holds true. People are changing church and some are even moving on to other faiths. In his book "A New Kind of Church" Aubrey Malphurs lists three core reasons why people are leaving:

People Think Differently

One reason is that they think differently than do people in the typical church. More than one half of America's congregations were established prior to World War II. They feel that many act as if they were still living in that period as noted by:

- America was a monocultural world
- America was largely white, Anglo-Saxon and Protestant or Catholic.
- Travel was difficult, and few people or conducted business overseas.
- Americans were not familiar with people from other countries and religions.[48]

He further states, modernism was the predominant worldview – and most people put their faith for a better world in *science* and *education.* The church of that day was challenged with the question: **Does God exist?** That world no longer exists! Today's person lives in:

- A multicultural world.
- Can travel to any part of the world with a click of the remote control on the television.
- They think the hope for a future lies in the poet, and artists rather than the scientist and educator.
- They feel that churches are set up to answer real-life questions that people are no longer asking.
- Many builders in the churches who were young prior to the 60's do not own a computer.
- The majority of the traditional churches in America are saying "come join us on our terms."
- Internet and other sources have exposed the average American to various other faiths – non Christian faiths, such as Judaism, Buddhism, Hinduism, and Islam.

- Fifty percent of those exploring faith online – use it to explore other faiths.
- A different question is asked today: **What God is real?**[49]

Faith is no longer tied to the Church

His second reason people no longer attend church is that their faith is inextricably tied to neither church nor to its leadership. This was true of the Builder generation in the early and mid-twentieth century:

- Early church attenders as well as the unchurched believed that people *"should arrive at their religious beliefs independent of any church or synagogue."*
- Further, one could be a good Christian or Jew without being a part of any Christian or Jewish faith community.
- Americans are individualists who pride themselves in their personal autonomy and can do what they want.
- Many Americans are individualists who are convinced that religious authority lies in the believer – not in the church, nor in the Bible, despite occasional claims of infallibility and inerrancy on the part of some.
- Another factor is one's prior exposure to church. Many of the boomer generation attended church when they were young because their builder parents took them. Yet many opted out once they graduated from high school.
- In contrast, a large number of the Busters and Mosaics have rarely attended church, if at all.
- Millions of adults have dropped out of church, not because they've lost interest in spiritual matters or are disconnecting from God – *but because they want more of God in their lives.*[50]

Sunday morning is no longer sacred

Malphurs' third reason people no longer attend church is that Sunday morning is no longer sacred. The church reached its highest attendance levels between 1954 and 1962, according to Gallup's statistics:

- For the Builder generation, church attendance offered respectability. Going to church was what proper middle-class people did on Sunday mornings, especially in the South.
- Participation in church concurred with an emphasis on the family.
- During that time in some parts of the country, American culture also became largely a churched culture.
- Church is what many people in the South and some parts of the North did on Sunday mornings.
- Some cities had "blue laws" that prohibited stores from opening on Sundays as well. For some people church was the only thing to do on Sundays.[51]
- However, all that changed in most of America. Sunday mornings are sacred no longer, and a number of rivals have surfaced to compete with the church for the hearts and souls of the American citizenry on Sunday.
- With the repeal of the "blue laws," stores can be open on Sunday as well as the other six days of the week. This means many Christians have to choose to work on Sunday or possibly face job loss:
- As a pastor in North Carolina during the 1980s, the church I was serving lost many of our young people to the fast food industry, the military and many working in major recreation, convenient stores had to sell alcoholic beverages on Sundays as part of their duties or lose their jobs.
- Today, two decades later it is accepted as normal for children to seek work permits in order to work on Sundays or any other day the job requires. Many of the fast food, convenient stores and even many merchandisers are open 24/7.
- In appealing to parents to keep the young people in church, their number one reason for allowing them to leave the church was economics. Another parent explained that it was important for them to work in order to learn how to meet the public. God forbid!
- I also had one church officer to resign because he would have to open his business early on Sundays.

- Other competitors for the church are sports, shopping malls, movies, cable TV, internet, and recreation facilities, area beaches and amusement parks.

One of our major priorities at the Bread of Life Ministries is targeting unchurched Christians – people who believe but do not belong and; we also prioritize the unchurched non-Christians concentrating on:

- Developing a Biblical worldview
- Kingdom growth over numerical growth.
- Provide multi-services, training, services and activities at times other than the traditional Sunday and Wednesday concepts.
- Top priority is small group concept of ministry.
- Instituting the teaching, training and practices necessary to re-introduce the priesthood of all believers concept of ministry!

People are looking for a word from God. They are not interested in our personal opinions and flying by the seat of our pants schemes. They want more than the latest political or public opinion commentary. Our people yearn for a message from God in this age of uncertainty and humanistic self-centeredness. In a time when the biblical family is being redefined through multi-divorces, single parenting, same-sex marriages and cohabitation – is there a Word from the Lord? Embedded within each depressing thirty-minute newscast are little terrorizing news shots. The news seems to be designed to add to the frustrations.

The people are hit with global, political, and economic instability. At the same time all of our institutions founded under a biblical consensus are subtly being changed before our eyes to a secular humanistic consensus. People need to know that their only hope is in Jesus Christ and His Word. The salt and light, [Christians] have got to hit the streets! Now, review the three reasons Americans aren't attending Church:

Three reasons Americans aren't attending Church

1. People think differently today.
2. A person's faith is no longer tied to the church.
3. Sunday morning is no longer sacred.[52]

According to Barna Group's 2014 tracking data, people offered a variety of answers for the present dilemma.

When asked, what if anything helps Americans grow in their faith?

- The people answered, prayer, family, and friends, reading the Bible, having children – but the church did not even crack the top-ten list.
- U.S. adults today are evenly divided on attending church. While half (49%) say it is *"somewhat" or "very" important* – the 51% say it is *"not too" or "not at all"* important.
- The research reflects that the divide between the religiously active and those resistant to churchgoing impacts American culture, morality, politics and religion.
- Future generations are not looking favorable at church attendance. Millennials (those 30 and under) stand out as the least likely to value church attendance – only 2 out of 10 believe it is important.
- More than one-third of Millennial adults (35%) take an anti-church stance. In contrast, Elders (those over 68) are the ideal of most likely (40%) to view church attendance as "very" important, compared to one-quarter (24%) who deem it "not at all" important.
- Boomers (ages 49-67) and Generation Xers (ages 30-48) fall in the middle of these polar opposites.[53]

While the debate rages about what will happen to Millenials as they get older:

- Will they return to church attendance later in life? They are starting at a lower baseline for church participation and commitment than previous generations of young adults.

Have you attended church in the past week?

- About four in ten Americans say "yes."
- 59% of Millenials who grew up in the church have dropped out at some point.

- The number of people who say they have not attended a church function at all in the past six months has increased considerably in the past 10 years. This is true particularly among younger Americans; more than half of the Millenials haven't been to church in at least six months.[54]

Who goes to church – and why?

- While tens of millions of Americans attend church each weekend, the practice has declined in recent years. According to the data overall church attendance has dipped from 43% in 2004 to 36% today. But beyond a dip in attendance numbers, the nature of churchgoing. Regular attenders use to be people who went to church three or more weekends each month – or even several times a week. Now people who show up once every four to six weeks consider themselves regular churchgoers. Many pastors and church leaders are reacting accordingly for sporadic attendance in their ministry planning.
- Furthermore, the percentage of people who have not attended a church function at all in the past six months has surged in the last decade from one-third to nearly two-fifths of all Americans. The shift is even more drastic among younger Americans: more than half of millennials and Generation Xers say they have not been to church in the last six months.[55]

Further the data reflects that millennials who are opting out of church cite three factors with equal weight in their decision:

- 35% cite church irrelevance, hypocrisy, and the moral failures of its leaders as reasons to check out of church altogether.
- Two out of ten unchurched millennials say they feel God is missing in church.
- And one out of ten senses that legitimate doubt is prohibited, starting at the front door.[56]

Perhaps more poignant than reasons not to turn up for church are the motivations of those who do believe church is very important and cite two reasons above the rest:

- (1) To be closer to God (44%) and (2) to learn about God (27%).
- One in five (22%) say they go to church because the Bible teaches fellowship with other believers.
- In spite of growing loneliness, just 1 in 10 reports going to church because they are looking for community.
- Although people cite their primary reasons for attending church as growing closer to God and learning more about Him, Barna Group finds closeness seldom happens.
- Fewer than one in 10 who has ever been to church say they learned something about God or Jesus the last time they attended in fact, the majority of people say they did not gain any significant or new insights regarding faith when they last attended church.[57]

Adults are aware of their very real spiritual needs, yet they are increasingly dissatisfied with the church's attempt to meet those spiritual needs and are turning elsewhere.

Postmodernism and the Word of God

In earlier sections I addressed compromise, assimilation and absolute truth. While the postmodern shift has opened doors for many, it has no doubt closed many. In postmodernity the "whatever" attitude is king; which leaves little room for absolute truth. Therefore, the modern thought is no longer accepted; and that creates a communications problem for many Christians. Those biblical truths that moderns have believed all their lives are questionable today with the postmoderns:

- The Bible is no longer accepted as the authoritative Word of God.
- Dogmatism is out.
- Jesus is no longer the unique Savior.
- Little belief in absolute truth.

- There's little acceptance of God's master plan for our lives.
- Most people today think when you die that's it, no future.

So the postmodern person might hear your rebuttal for these untruths, but that will depend heavily on how you present it. If you are going to be dogmatic about them don't engage yourself. There were educators in my family, so one thing I remember all of them going off to summer school each year so they could remain current and relevant with their students. Many pastors and others in leadership to the lowest level do not feel that this matter of "relevancy" is important enough even to look into, but in the meantime they are wringing their hands wondering why so many are leaving the traditional and institutional churches. What are we to do?

Think Missionary

It is quite obvious that the individual church of the twenty-first century will have to compete with the rivals mentioned above and other new forms at the same time. Many progressive, biblically-oriented Christians are reaching out for new ways to minister. One of the reasons for demanding new concepts of church ministry is the accelerated rate of change in our society. Some see this as a threat while others accept it as a challenge! There is a saying, "the church lags about forty years behind in making those changes necessary to remain relevant in the ever changing society. If that is true, then many of our churches around the country are operating a late seventies concept of doing church along with that era's thought. Imagine the pastor preaching one of his father's sermons from the 70's this coming Sunday morning without making any changes or adjustments. As terrible as that may seem, those pastors who do not remain current with the times are doing just that. Speaking authoritatively from the 70's to the postmoderns – is speaking from antiquity since we are no longer living in modern time.

As the result of urbanization, mobilization, internet, media, education, government, and medicine, many are experiencing completely new life styles. The country is going through a great transition; and that means the church will have to move out of the four walls to represent Christ in the world through service. In some respects we ought to welcome change for it can make life better and more interesting. Too much and untimed change creates very serious problems. It separates young and old, the informed and the ignorant, the leadership and the followship.

With the unchanging divine guidance of the Holy Spirit and the Word of God, the Christian community can face up to change collectively. Biblical answers are not always apparent, but God never fails to fulfill His promise to honor those who search diligently.

Historical records show over and over again that men and women whose lives have been guided by Scripture have, in the long run, contributed most to cultural progress.

But change we must – because a *restored* priesthood of ministers has risen up in this nation. I will cover this restored minister fully in chapter 13. He or she may come from the streets, prison, the professions or traditional churches steeped in orthodoxy, but they are not what the local churches expected. While, this restored priesthood of ministers does not represent the majority of church members – it is equally clear, as I recorded in an earlier section, that they represent a significant and growing number of persons who have taken Christianity out of the church buildings and into the streets and marketplace. However, some among the restored priesthood of ministers seem to be upsetting the status quo of what has been accepted Christian morality for centuries.

Those churches unwilling to re-think and make necessary changes in their present methodology and concept of church will actually find themselves in a non-productive condition. God still speaks with a voice of hope! Are we listening? We had better hear what the Spirit is saying to the churches.

While serving in the military it was mandatory that we provide specialized training for all soldiers deploying to locations outside of the United States for peace or war. The training focused on familiarizing the soldier with the customs, culture, language and other demographics of not only the country to which they were going, but also the specific region and city or town in which they to be stationed. In Bible school those persons going to the mission field received this type of training. Most of us were in the pastoral ministry track expecting to work with churches in this country; so a fundamental course in foreign mission met the requirement for us.

My wife and I had the opportunity to actually work on the foreign mission field with missionaries from America and other countries for three years in Panama during the 70s' and two years in South Korea during the 80s.' The concept that I became familiar with in both instances took the ministry to the streets; that is, the ministry revolved around the people's availability rather than an ordained minister per se.

For sixteen years we have taught this concept in the Bread of Life Bible Institute which we founded for the specific purpose to "Equip for Ministry." Thus, we believe in and promote the priesthood of all believers; therefore every student is a priest [minister]. For more details on this concept see my books, *"Behold the Man"* and *"Drawn Away."* Wherever, we plant a Bible Institute; we end up fellowshipping with an area church [like-minded in theology and concept of ministry] already established there or we plant one.

Unlike the people who play the church rotation game; there is a much larger group of people who desire more than the average church has to offer. They are seeking more of the Truth [Jesus!]. Their desire is to develop their spirituality. Many paraministries are involved in the ministry of authentic spirituality.

Our culture is changing so fast that many pastors are either finding a comfort zone in the traditional concept and complaining about their empty pews or stepping down. However, I encourage them to stay on board, keep learning and make the necessary methodical changes to meet the challenges and needs of the postmodern world in which we find ourselves today. If your focus is wrong, secularism coupled with our fast rising globalized society, multiculturalism and humanism will over take you; just as it has consumed our institutions especially the media and academia will really rattle you.

I believe the Lord has brought the body of Christ to a place wherein the lines are clearly drawn. As believers, we have no authority to compromise or confuse God's Word – but rightly divide it is the only way for true believers. The Holy Spirit is His representative to the body to lead and guide us in all things. During modern time, most churches leaned on science, reason and legalism; however, we readily see that they are not acceptable to the new world of postmodernism that seeks clarity and reliability. Authentic Christianity is the only hope:

- You must be born again.
- Your worship to be accepted must be in Spirit and in truth.
- Your walk must be in the Spirit if we are to overcome the flesh.
- The Word of God has to be a lamp unto your feet and a light unto your path.
- You are a new creation in Christ. Our mind must be renewed.
- You must have a biblical worldview.
- You must adhere to sound doctrine.

Unless we are led by the Spirit of God change can be dangerous. In fact much of the ongoing change is in the wrong direction. Instead of a future-oriented people many are appearing, a present secular-oriented people, focused only on the here and now. While methods change biblical truths remain the same. The apostles' doctrine remains our starting point of reference. If we stick with the Spirit and the truth of God's Word – He will keep us from falling into compromise and assimilation.

In his book, *Preaching to a Postmodern World,* Graham Johnson declares, "What exists in the speaker's mind and in the listener's mind may not be the same thing." Further, the postmodern movement originated in debate over the use of language and interpretation. The battlefield has shifted. He further states that during the fifties through the seventies the inerrancy debate raged in what was labeled "The Battle for the Bible." Johnson points out the following dangerous issues:

- The real issue today is not of an inerrant text – as much as not having any text at all.
- The issue is no longer about what is in the text or what the original author intended but about what is in the interpretation of the text as understood by the present reader.
- The postmodern mistrust of words and text will put new pressure on the field of hermeneutics, particularly at the professional theological level.
- There are some theological teachers who will swallow the deconstructionist line – where any objective truth, history or

meaning is emptied from the text, the meaning becoming a matter of what readers construct for themselves.

- The biblical communicator who succumbs to this hermeneutic relinquishes speaking for God.[58]

When we lose divine revelation – all that remains
is human speculation and uncertainty.

These suspicions about language, which are subtle but persuasive, represent significant obstacles for communication. No Christian should ever want to abandon their passionate commitment to the truth. As Christians our offensive weapon is the Sword of the Spirit, the Bible. We must be wise in wielding it tactfully in communications with the postmoderns' view of biblical texts as relative and authority as oppressive.

We must remember unlike the moderns; the postmodern listeners do not want the Christian to demand that they believe, at least not without adequate time to fully process what's communicated. Dr. Johnson offers ten distinctives that emerges as hallmarks of postmodern people:

1. They're reacting to modernity and all its tenets.
2. They reject objective truth.
3. They're skeptical and suspicious of authority.
4. They're like missing persons in search of a self and identity.
5. They've blurred morality and are into whatever's expedient.
6. They continue to search for the transcendent.
7. They're living in a media world unlike any other.
8. They'll engage in the knowing smirk.
9. They're on a quest for community.
10. They live in a very material world.[59]

Not only is the communicator responsible for laying out the truth of God's Word but also to assist the listener's struggle to find the truth for his or herself.

I'm afraid that we often lead people to the misconception there's no room for doubt and questioning in the church. As believers we must allow people the permission to test the teaching before belief or they will stay away. We challenge the listener, but we insure them absolute freedom of choice!

STUDY GUIDE: CHAPTER 11

1. One of the major concerns facing churches today is
   _____.

2. The Church must change; however some things _____
   _____ change.

3. In a "New Kind of Church," Audrey Malphurs lists three reasons
   why people are leaving the Church. Briefly comment on each of
   the three reasons below:
   a.
   b.
   c.

4. The majority of traditional churches in America are saying,
   "_____" on our terms.

5. Many early church attendees felt one could be a good Christian
   or Jew without being a part of any Christian or Jewish
   _____.

6. A large _____ of busters and mosaics have
   _____ attended church at all.

7. People are looking for a _____ God.

8. People need to know that their only hope is _____
   _____.

9. The _____ prohibited businesses opening on Sundays.

10. The Christian worldview has been replaced in our culture with a
    _____ worldview.

11. The monocultural world has been replaced by a _____
    world.

12. A different question is asked about God today, _____
    _____?

13. List three reasons why people are leaving the church:
    1.
    2.
    3.

14. Why is re-thinking the church important?

15. According to Barna research, adults who believe church is very important cite two reasons above the rest: _____ and _____.

CHAPTER 12

YES WE CAN!

The leaders of the Protestant Reformation *rediscovered* and *redefined* the role of the laity as all of God's people involved in the life and mission of the church. Martin Luther, the chief leader of the Reformation championed the general priesthood of all believers. The church needs faithful men and women who passionately desire to move beyond marginal church membership to disciples in action – thus recovering the dynamic supernatural powerful witness of the early Christians as recorded in the Book of Acts.

Christianity is steadily being pushed to the margin of a now secularized [no God] or multicultural [multi-god] American society. Church history reveals that during the Middle Ages and Reformation period there was a *sacralization of life.* In spite of the advancement of the sacred – the 20th century brought with it a *secularization of life.* Now, following the path of the 20th century; we are experiencing in the 21st century an advanced *secularized life* of unprecedented proportions. On the other hand, many people are presently searching for *renewal principles* for their lives.

No longer business as Usual

No local church or church body can afford to continue on with the same business and programs as usual. In so doing that particular community forfeits their God-given mission of effectively ministering the Gospel of Jesus Christ to the people of this postmodern age. All local churches must recover the dynamic supernatural powerful witness of the early Christians. *Yes we can!* It requires making the Gospel relevant. Today these two questions are asked:

1. Has the Gospel lost its relevance? The answer is a resounding NO!
2. Has the church lost its relevance? The answer for too often is an unqualified yes!

Certainly it is not because the Gospel is no longer true. It is because the institutional church in varying degrees has lost its sense of mission *through all of its members to all of its community.* As the relevance or lack of it is so evident, we should realize that people are changing; and we are living in a radically postmodern age. Technology is producing a new person [the postmodern]. The church must find an effective way of reaching this postmodern person.

The price of fuel for our cars is on the rise and everyone owning or operating an automobile are experiencing the affect. We are told that the increase is due to required *retooling* at the refinery to change over to the summer grades. Some people grumble, but everyone who wants to keep driving their automobile has to pay the price.

If the church is going to regain its relevance and rightful place in society, it will have to retool. Like the refinery the churches must changeover for another season. If there is no changeover of the gas for summer, the car may crank, but run erratically because a very necessary component is absent from the fuel for the engine to run properly and efficiently.

As the people of God, Christians are His representatives in today's world. We had better hear what the Spirit is saying to the churches! He is reminding us to get His people back on mission and *retool* by putting the true Gospel of Christ *back* into the hands of the people and send them to this generation and to those to come. That calls for a return to the New Testament concept of the church; not as a highly organized institution but as a Christian community where every member is a minister witnessing for Christ in every walk and station of life.

A Biblically-based Ministry

The pastoral office involves application of the Gospel to the community and society in a way that makes the church relevant with the rapidly increasing social changes being experienced worldwide today. One major change that must take place is that, pastors must stop going it alone! He or she must bring *all* the church with them. The pastor is an *equipper* and that requires more than a Sunday morning sermon and Wednesday night with the faithful few. It is so sad that such a basic doctrine as, *"the priesthood of all believers"* must be rediscovered and renewed by every new generation of Christians. Let's review several verses which establish this doctrine:

"And He Himself gave some to be **apostles**, *some* **prophets**, *some* **evangelists**, *and some* **pastors** for the **equipping** of the saints:

- for the work of ministry,
- for the **edifying** of the body of Christ,
- till we all come to the **unity of the faith,**
- and the **knowledge of the Son of God,**
- **to a perfect man,**

"**….. to the measure of the stature of the fullness of Christ.**" (Ephesians 4:11-12)

Three stages of growth are presented here. Gifted leaders are responsible for the *equipping of the saints.* The saints are to be trained:

1. To do *the work of ministry;*
2. The goal being – *body of Christ* is built up.
3. The final goal – achieve maturity, truth, and love.

In 1 Peter 2:4-10, the foundational Scripture for this doctrine, we read: *Coming to Him as to a living stone, rejected indeed by men, but chosen by God and precious, you also, as living stones, are being built up a spiritual house, a* **holy priesthood,** *to offer up spiritual sacrifices acceptable to God through Jesus Christ. Therefore it is also contained in the Scripture,*

"Behold, I lay in Zion
A chief cornerstone, elect, precious,
And he who believes on Him will by
No means be put to shame."

Therefore, to you who believe, He is precious, but to those who are disobedient,

> *The stone which the builders*
> *rejected*
> *has become the chief cornerstone*
> *and*
> *A stone of stumbling*
> *And a rock of offense."*

They stumble, being disobedient to the word, to which they also were appointed. But you are a chosen generation, a royal priesthood, a holy nation, His own special people, that you may proclaim the praises of Him who called you out of darkness into His marvelous light; who once were not a people but are now the people of God, who had not obtained mercy but now have obtained mercy.

In his book, *The Priesthood of All Believers,* Oscar E. Feucht says, "Jesus who was rejected of men has become the Cornerstone of the church. And all believers have become living Stones built into that temple. The Holy Spirit is the Architect. The Christians themselves are building blocks. In verse 5 the figure of speech changes. *The believers are the priests* offering themselves to God in daily service, in their "wholeness," that is in all that they are, do, and say.[60]

Christians have been entrusted with the greatest enterprise in the world. That is something in each person that God yearns to own, to inhabit, and to use. There is something He wants from every individual, namely, loyalty, fellowship, and obedience.

Fulfilling the Old Testament

Feucht states, there is a unique correspondence between the Old Testament and New Testament regarding the priesthood of all believers. The prophet Jeremiah speaks of a new age for all the people of God. *"I [God] will put My law within them, and I will write it upon their hearts; and I will be their God, and they shall be My people"* (Jeremiah 31:31-33). The Book of Hebrews indicates that the Old Testament rites were temporary *until all of God's people would form the **priesthood** of the new covenant* (Hebrews 8:8, 10).

In 2 Corinthians 6:16, the Apostle Paul quotes Ezekiel 37:27. *"I* [the Lord] *will live in them* and *among them,* and I will be their God and *they shall be My people."* In his letter to Titus he speaks of Christ "who gave Himself for us to redeem us from all iniquity and to *purify for Himself a people of His own* who are zealous for good deeds" (Titus 2:14).

Isaiah predicted the New Testament era when *all* of God's people would be His servants: *"You shall be called **the priests of the Lord,** and men shall speak of you as the **ministers of our God"*** (61:6).

The Witness of Paul and John

In his dissertation on the use of the gifts of the Spirit, Paul says, "So we, though many, are one body in Christ, and individually members one of another. Having gifts that differ …… let us use them" (Romans 12:4-6). "Do you not know that you are God's temple?"

(1 Corinthians 3:6). God does not live in man-made buildings but in persons. The Book of Revelation at a number of places echoes the **priesthood** of every Christian. God "loved us, and by His death He has freed us from our sins and made us *a kingdom of priests* to serve our God" (5:9-10).

The Christian's heart is God's altar.

At the resurrection, the faithful believers "shall be *priests of God* and of Christ, and they will rule with Him." (20:6)

Contagious Witnesses

When the serious Christian compares what is happening in contemporary society with the history of declining societies he or she becomes desperate about the ongoing present condition of humanity. The true impact of Jesus Christ in the world is the *collective influence of individual Christians* **right where they are** day in and day out. Laborers, teachers, politicians, students, athletes, clerks, executives, doctors, lawyers .... quietly, steadily, continually and consistently infecting the world where they live with a contagious witness of the contemporary Christ and His relevance to life.

In order to avoid the national disaster of moral bankruptcy for which we are heading, vast numbers must be reconciled to God through Christ and become dedicated to the expansion of the Kingdom. To fulfill this mission every Christian should be captivated by the challenge of knowing that he or she has something:

- Not to be stored up, but to be scattered – right where you are.
- Not to be defended, but to be declared – right where you are.
- Not to be conserved, but to be communicated – right where you are.

God's declaration in the Old Testament is as true today as in that day: It is *"not by might nor by power, but by My Spirit,' says the Lord Almighty"* (Zechariah 4:6). From the very first sermon of the Christian era, preached by Peter on the Day of Pentecost, slick and clever methodology were not deployed to bring 3000 converts into the church; God did it through a very unlikely fisherman named Peter. Homiletics experts would probably find the message and the messenger unacceptable.

Yet, think of the impact on the local society and culture of these new witnesses for Christ and His kingdom. All this came through the power and work of the Holy Spirit. Jesus said, "whoever believes in Me, as the Scripture has said, *streams of living water will flow from within him.'* By this He meant the Spirit, whom those who believed in Him were to receive" (John 7:38-39).

This overflow is what brings blessings to people; and remember nothing is too hard for God! The gospel of Christ through the power of the Holy Spirit can transform the hardest cases imaginable. ***"But you shall receive power after the Holy Spirit has come unto you"*** (Acts 1:8).

STUDY GUIDE: CHAPTER 12

1. The leaders of the Protestant Reformation _____ and _____ the role of the laity.

2. Chief leaders of the Reformation championed the general _____ of all _____.

3. During the Reformation period, there was a_____ of life. The 20th century brought a _____ of life. The 21st century brought a_____ secularized life.

4. All local churches must _____ the dynamic _____ powerful witness of the early church.

5. The people of God are His _____ in today's world.

6. A Christian community where every member is a _____ requires a return to the New Testament concept _____ the _____.

7. One major change that must take place is that _____ must stop going it alone.

8. The saints must be equipped for the work of the _____ and for the _____ of the body of Christ.

9. Three stages of growth for the Christian is presented in Ephesians 4:11-12: (1) (2) (3)

10. _____ is the foundational Scripture for the doctrine of the priesthood of all believers.

11. Hebrews 8:8 says, God's people would form the _____ of the new covenant.

12. Isaiah 61:6 sys, "You shall be called the _____ of the _____."

13. Each believer has _____ (Romans 12:4-6).

14. The impact of Jesus Christ in the world is the _____ of individual Christians right where they are day in and day out.

15. Pentecost was accomplished through the _____ and _____ of the Holy Spirit.

CHAPTER 13

PRUNING FOR MORE FRUIT

Over the past several years, I have encountered many within the body of Christ who are going through a process of pruning. I first noticed this happening in my own life and the Bread of Life Ministries I oversee. I then began to hear from many others in the body of Christ who are experiencing similar challenges, feeling that they are being "cut back."

The True Vine

"I am the true vine, and My Father is the vinedresser. Every branch in Me that does not bear fruit He takes away; and every branch that bears fruit He prunes, that it may bear more fruit" (John 15:1, 2).

Through the extended metaphor of the vine and the branches, Jesus set forth the standard of Christian living. Jesus used the imagery of agricultural life at that time; i.e. vines and vine crops. He specifically identified Himself as the "true vine" and the Father as the "vinedresser" or caretaker of the vine. The vine has two types of branches:

- Branches that bear fruit (vv. 2, 8).
- Branches that do not bear fruit (vv. 2, 6).

The branches that bear fruit are genuine believers. Every branch that bears fruit He prunes, that it may bear more fruit. Every branch that does not bear fruit *He takes away.*

According to this passage – *pruning is **not** punishment for bad branches!* Just the opposite, it is for those branches that are bearing fruit. Branches that are unfruitful are *cut off altogether,* while the care of the Vinedresser is reserved for those branches He sees are already fruitful.

If you are one of the many in the body of Christ who is going through a pruning process right now, *praise God!* God is pruning your branches in order to bring in order to *bring a greater harvest.* In these challenging times, God is cutting back or pruning us from what is unnecessary in order to put us through a greater and more painful experience to be more fruitful to the kingdom.

Fit to fight

In any operation requiring manpower, it is necessary to tailor the force to fit the mission at hand. God put Gideon's army through various paces to tailor them down to what satisfied Him. The force He now has is fit to fight and win the battle. Too many would be stumbling over one another trying to steal the glory. Jude has a word for each the fruitful and the unfruitful.

He offers a very encouraging word to those fruitful left on the vine to maintain your life in the Lord: *"Building yourselves up on your most holy faith, praying in the Holy Spirit. "Keep yourselves in the love of God, looking for the mercy of our Lord Jesus Christ unto eternal life"* (vv.20, 21).

True Christians have a **sure** foundation (see 1 Corinthians 3:11) and cornerstone (see Ephesians 2:20) in Christ Jesus. The truths of the Christian faith have been provided in the teaching of the truths of God's Word; so that the Christian builds him or herself up by

- The Word of God (see Acts 20:32).
- Praying in the Holy Spirit (see Ephesians 6:18).

This idea of "building ourselves up" connotes the idea of spiritual readiness. Years ago in the military in order to stay fit, we would build ourselves up by lifting weights, jogging, swimming or other exercises, and we would also restrict ourselves from certain foods and social activities – all for the sake of keeping our physical bodies in the best shape possible.

In these postmodern times, how much more are we called to be spiritually fit! We must be fit soldiers who are growing in our faith, living a life of prayer and walking in love. And yet to do this requires what seems to the natural mind a paradox. The more God prunes us from what is unnecessary for us – the fitter we become. As God cuts back or prunes, it's always with the goal to build us up.

Branches that are unfruitful are cut off altogether!

Cloud without Water

Writing in anticipation of the increase and rise of [unfruitful branches] false teachers' and apostates' attacks on the name of Jesus Christ and His Church – indeed, we live in such a day. Jude said,

*"These are spots in your love feasts, while they feast with you without fear, serving only themselves. They are clouds without water, carried about by the winds; late autumn trees without fruit, twice dead, pulled by the roots; raging waves of the sea, foaming up their own shame; wandering stars for whom is reserved the blackness of darkness **forever"** (vv. 12, 13).*

These apostates were [and are today] dirty spots, filth on the garment of the church. They promise spiritual life, but they are empty clouds; which brings the hope of rain, but actually deliver nothing but dryness and death (see Proverbs 25:14). An apostate is a *defector from the truth:*

- Someone who has known the truth.
- Someone who has given some show of affirmation to it.
- Perhaps even proclaimed it for a while.
- In the end they reject the truth.
- Opposes the truth and undermines it.
- He or she is a traitor to the faith and secretly an enemy, but stays with the church.
- Actively seeks acceptance among the people of God.
- Because everything they do undermines faith and corrupts the truth, such persons pose a dangerous threat to the health and welfare of the flock.

- They bend over backward to appear friendly, likable and **pious.** That is why Jesus compares them to ravenous wolves in sheep's clothing (see Matthew 7:15).
- A few apostates are outspoken and aggressive in their opposition to the truth, but most are subtler.
- Others may actually start out meaning well, but they never get past being *double-minded.* They are like seeds sprouting in shallow or weedy soil. Their own shallowness or worldliness makes it impossible for God's Word to take root (see Matthew 13:20-22).
- Despite whatever temporary appearance of spiritual life they might display, they are *incapable of producing real fruit,* and they eventually fall away.

Don't be fooled by the temporary appearance of spiritual life and health in the beginning. When such a person abandons the faith, it proves he or she was always unregenerate, unbelieving, and still in their sins. Jude 19 says, these apostate teachers are sensual persons; and provides a profile of an apostate:

1. Ungodly (v.4)
2. Morally perverted (v.4)
3. Deny Christ (v.4)
4. Defile the flesh (v.8)
5. Rebellious (v.8)
6. Revile holy angels (v.8)
7. Dreamers (v.10)
8. Ignorant (v.10)
9. Corrupted (v.10)
10. Grumblers (v.16)
11. Fault finders (v.16)
12. Self-seeking (v.16)
13. Arrogant speakers (v.16)
14. Flatterers (v.16)
15. Mockers (v.18)
16. Cause division (v.19)
17. Worldly minded (v.19)
18. **Without the Spirit** (v.19)

When false teaching goes unchallenged, it breeds more confusion and draws still more shallow and insincere people into the fold!

Obviously, these people hurt the cause of truth tremendously. People who embrace apostasy are destroyed by it. Notice five out of the seven churches in Revelation 2-3, were either beginning to defect from *the faith* or were already apostates. Sardis was already apostate and Laodicia moving quickly toward final rejection of truth. Christ's central message to all but two of the churches included a mandate to deal with apostates in their midst.

The battle for **truth** in the church has always been very difficult – but a very necessary conflict.

Apostasy is a real and present danger in the churches today as always. Actually, more dangerous than ever because:

- Most Christians today don't care about the presence of false doctrine.
- Most Christians today don't take is seriously nor see it their duty to fight against apostasy.
- They want open inclusivity, tolerance and acceptance of opposing ideas.
- Many Christians are rejecting the few key gospel doctrines regarded as absolutely essential to true Christianity.

A great number of church leaders today, are far more likely to express their displeasure and indignation at someone who calls for doctrinal clarity and accuracy than to firmly oppose some self-styled apostate who is attacking some vital truth of God's Word.

Though they know better, many of our local churches are bowing to pressure and elevating good works over sound doctrine – insisting that truly good works are the fruit of faith. Not so! Take another look at chapter 6 of this book.

Speaking the Truth

Today those who love to speak the truth of God's Word are not liked. But we cannot let that stop us from the kingdom's work we are **all** called to do:

- Speaking His word and sharing His love.
- We cannot be discouraged or deterred by what we see around us and retreat to the four walls disengaging from the culture and world that so desperately need to see the light.
- Things that were unimaginable twenty years ago are now the norm. This is true within the church and in the culture around us.
- We must not let these things stop us from moving forward.
- It is in these challenging moments that we can let our training and preparation count for the Lord.

STUDY GUIDE: CHAPTER 13

1. What is meant by "cutting back" in the text of this chapter?

2. Pruning is not _____.

3. What is the term Jude uses for the _____ and the unrighteous?

4. List several characteristics of an apostate: _____
    _____.

5. Name the two churches that were already apostates in chapter 2-3 of the Book of Revelation when the Apostle John began to write the Revelation: _____.

6. Most Christians are indifferent to false teaching today. T. or F.

7. Jesus identified Himself as the _____ and the Father as the _____.

8. Pruning _____
    punishment.

9. The idea of "building ourselves up" connotes the idea of _____.

10. Unfruitful branches are _____.

11. An apostle is a _____ from the truth.

12. Apostates are _____ of producing real fruit.

13. "Without the Spirit" is characteristic of the _____.

14. Most Christians are rejecting the _____
_____ doctrines regarded as
absolutely essential to true Christianity.

15. Today those who speak the truth of God's Word are not
_____.

CHAPTER 14

FORWARD AND UPWARD

In this chapter we will see that a disciple is a learner and a witness. If you belong to a typical church, it contains people who believe that if they get to church in time to hear the sermon on Sunday morning, they have fulfilled their weekly Christian obligation. So they can depart satisfied.

People who practice such Christianity do not understand the nature of the church or the nature of the faith they profess. First of all being a disciple of Christ means more than attending a weekly sermon, and Bible study. Though that person is hearing and receiving truth – they are similar to the Dead Sea which has inlets, but no outlets; truth received only, with no outlets to life and others dies! We hear people say, "Our church is a Word Church," another proclaims "We are a church of love." If they cannot say they are both, then that church is not operating fully in "the faith."

The Household of Faith

The fact of the matter is, when you became a part of God's family and join the household of faith, you inherit a house full of sisters and brothers. Therefore there will be the normal sibling rivalry with some, and others who make life quite difficult, but we don't quit! Being a disciple [a learner and witness] we meet these challenges through Christ's answer – love [*agape*] for one another. There are approximately fifty of these "one another" ministries. Listed below are a few of them as found throughout the New Testament. I have extracted four major exhortations [in bold print] that are critical to the relational aspects of authentic discipleship:

"Love one another" (John 13:35).

"Be at peace with one another" (Mark 9:50).
"Wash one another's feet" (John 13:14).
"Be devoted to one another in brotherly love" (Romans 12:10).
"Honor one another above yourselves" (Romans 12:10).
"Stop passing judgment on one another" (Romans 14:13).
"Accept one another, just as Christ accepted you" (Romans 15:7).
"Instruct one another" (Romans 15:14).
"Greet one another with a holy kiss"(Romans 16:16).
"When you come together to eat, wait for one another" (1 Corinthians 11:33).
"Have equal concern for one another" (1 Corinthians 12:25).
"Serve one another in love" (Galatians 5:18; 2 Corinthians 4:5).
"If you keep on biting and devouring one another … you will be destroyed by each other" (Galatians 5:15).
"Let us not be conceited provoking and envying one another" (Galatians 5:26).
"Teach one another" (Colossians 3:16).
"Admonish one another" (Colossians 3:16).
"Make your love increase and overflow for one another" (1 Thessalonians 3:12).
"Build up one another" (1 Thessalonians 5:11; Ephesians 4:2).
"Encourage one another daily" (1 Thessalonians 4:18; 5:11).
"Spur one another on toward love and good deeds" (Hebrews 10:24).
"Do not slander one another" (James 4:11).
"Do not grumble against one another" (James 5:9).
"Confess your sins one to another" (James 5:16).
"Pray for one another" (James 5:16).
"Love one another deeply from the heart" (1 Peter 1:22).
"Offer hospitality to one another without grumbling" (1 Peter4:9).
"Each one should use whatever gift he [or she] has received to serve one another" (1 Peter 4:10).
"Clothe yourself with humility toward one another" (1 Peter 5:5).
"Fellowship with one another" (1 John 1:5-7).

It is obvious that these one another ministries operating in the body of Christ are important to God, since He speaks of them so frequently.

Practicing "one another ministries" is expected of all true disciples of Christ. I have highlighted four that are critical to authentic discipleship, though all the others are embedded within them:

Love One Another

The first "one another" ministry is found in John 13:34-35, Jesus said,

"A new commandment I give to you, that you love one another, even as I have loved you, that you also love one another. By this all men will know that you are My disciples, if you have love one for another."

In 1 Corinthians 13:1-3, Paul said in essence, it doesn't matter what you may do in Christian service, or sacrifices, or even the giving of your very life's blood, if you don't have love for one another *[individually]* and *[corporately]* everything else is actually a waste of time. If you are going to do something for God, love must be the motivation. Notice the position of chapter 13, the love chapter in conjunction with chapter 12 where the gifts of the Spirit are identified and listed, and chapter 14 where the operation of the gifts are clarified.

Before they are operated, the gifts must pass through love (chapter 13), which I believe activates them for the glory of God. The apostle Paul is also credited with the profound passage, *"Love is the fulfilling of the Law"* (Romans 13:10).

The Apostle John identifies loving one another as absolutely **basic** to living for Christ and advancing His kingdom   (see 1 John 3:11).

Jesus said breaking one of the laws made that individual guilty of breaking all of them. Indicating the keeping of every law was impossible; however, He said, "If you love Me you will unconsciously fulfill all of them." In other words, take any commandment; if the person loves God, you don't have to tell him or her: *"You shall have no other gods before Me."* Nor would this person ever think of *"Taking the Lord's name in vain."* Love would fulfill all of these laws regarding God. At the same time, if the person loves others as he or she loves themselves. They would not have to be told to honor their father and mother. Their love for them would allow nothing less. Loving his or her neighbor would negate any thought of coveting what belongs to their neighbor.

You would only offend such a one by telling them they should not steal from or bear false witness against their neighbor. These sins would not cross his or her mind. That's love. Notice the characteristics of that kind of love (Gk. "agape"):

- **It suffers long** – is patient (1 Thessalonians 5:14).
- **It is kind** – gentle especially with those who hurt (Ephesians 4:32).
- **It does not envy** – is not jealous of what others have (Proverbs 23:17).
- **It does not act rudely** – mean –spiritedly, insulting others (Ecclesiastes 5:2).
- **It does not parade itself** – put itself on display (John 3:30).
- **It does not seek its own** – way, or act pushy (1 Corinthians 10:24).
- **It is not provoked** – or angered (Proverbs 19:11).
- **It thinks no evil** – does not keep score on others (Hebrews 10:17).
- **It rejoices not in iniquity** – takes no pleasure when others fall into sin (Mark 3:5).
- **It rejoices in the truth** – is joyful when righteousness prevails (2 John 4).
- **It bears all things** – handles the burdensome (Galatians 6:2).
- **It believes all things** – trusts in God no matter what (Proverbs 3:5).
- **It hopes all things** – keeps looking up, does not despair (Philippians 3:15).
- **It endures all things** – puts up with everything; does not wear out (Galatians 6:9).
- **It never fails** – the only thing it cannot do is fail (1 Corinthians 16:14).

The gifts of the Spirit are temporary and for this age, while we are children (v. 11). Not so with love; which continues into the ages to come it is eternal, complete and fulfilling. All manifestations of the Spirit must at the same time manifest the ways of love, for love is the ultimate issue behind all things.

Serve One Another in Love (Galatians 5:13)

The second "one another" ministry is "serve one another." Jesus was the supreme example of a servant. The King of Kings and Lord of Lords relinquished His privileges and gave His life as a selfless sacrifice in serving others:

- He pleased not Himself.
- He did not seek high places of the world.
- He did not choose a life of ease, comfort, and pleasure.
- He went about doing good – and He cared for the needs of the sick and poor.
- He looked upon the things of others our helplessness, our danger, our need for a Savior.
- He cared for the souls of all.

In Galatians 5:13, Paul puts forth an argument opposite to that of legalism concerning liberty. Unlike their claims to circumcision and the law, he points out that true Christian liberty is the freedom to serve one another in life.

If I have no love for others and no desire to serve
others – I should question whether Christ is really
in my life. Am I really saved or deceived?

The Holy Spirit through undeserved favor called Paul to be an apostle and gave him spiritual authority. He also gives each believer at least one spiritual gift or supernatural endowment and power to love others; so that he or she can fulfill their gift (s) in the body of Christ (see 1 Corinthians 12:7, 11). God works in believers to benefit the *entire* body, not just individual Christians (vv. 25, 26). Various gifts are distributed to bring diversity among the whole body, even as the human body has many parts having different functions:

THE WORD OF KNOWLEDGE/ TEACHER (1 Corinthians 12:7; Ephesians 4:11)

This gift is the special ability discover, analyze, and clearly clarify ideas which are pertinent to the growth and wellbeing of the body i.e "not wavering" (1 Corinthians 12:8; Ephesians 4:13-14).

THE WORD OF WISDOM (1 Corinthians 12:7, 8)

This gift is the special ability to know the mind of the Holy Spirit in such a way as to receive insight into how given knowledge may best be applied to specific needs arising in the body of Christ "ask" (James 1:5-6).

FAITH 1 Corinthians 12:8)

This gift is the special ability to discern with extraordinary confidence the will and purpose of God for the future of His work. [For all Christians] i.e. "move mountain" (Matthew 17:14-21).

MIRACLES (1 Corinthians 12:10, 28)

This gift is the special ability to serve as intermediaries through whom it pleases God to perform powerful acts that are perceived by observers to have altered the ordinary course of nature. i.e. "Tabitha" (Acts 9:36-41)

PROPHECY (1 Corinthians 12:10; Ephesians 4:11)

This gift is the special ability to receive and communicate an immediate message of God to His people through a divinely-appointed utterance. i.e. "Agabus" (Acts 21:10, 11)

DISCERNING OF SPIRITS (1 Corinthians 12:10)

This gift is the special ability that the Spirit give to certain members of the body of Christ [all mature Christians should have] to know with assurance whether certain behavior purported to be of God is in reality divine, human or satanic (see 1 Corinthians 6:1-6; 1 Thessalonians 5:19-22)

INTERPRETATION OF TONGUES (1 Corinthians 12:10)

This gift is the special ability to explain or translate the tongues spoken in the congregation so that the entire group might know what the message of one who speaks in tongues.

Again, a spiritual gift is a specific grace empowerment given to each true Christian directly by the Spirit of God. It is important that we understand that these gifts are not hereditary nor do we generate them ourselves; they are imparted to us by the Spirit Himself. The spiritual gift imparted to us by the Holy Spirit, I believe it is more a job description in the body of Christ, the church than a title.[61]

Restore one another (1 Thessalonians 5:11; Ephesians 4:2)

This is a very important part of holistic ministry; it demands that we bear the burden of an erring brother or sister in a manner that he or she is restored to fellowship with the faith community. Paul exhorts,

"Brethren, if a man [or woman] is overtaken in any trespass, you who are spiritual restore such a one in a spirit of gentleness, considering yourself lest you also be tempted. Bear one another's burdens, and so fulfill the law of Christ" (Galatians 6:1, 2).

Any trespass probably referring to the "sins of the flesh" in 5:19-21. Overtaken means "caught" in sin. The word "restore" means to mend. Mending the net was what John was doing when Jesus called him. Since the Reformation I believe that has been one of the main tasks facing church leadership – and certainly a much neglected task today.

There are members of the body of Christ who get caught off guard in sin probably at a vulnerable point. This person needs to be approached with gentleness (5:23) by fellow believers. Many times those not filled with the Spirit tend to intimidate the fallen believer by comparing themselves to the fallen person (vv. 3, 4). From time to time a doctor can catch a disease from a patient, so one restoring a fallen sinner is subject to getting "caught" in sin themselves if not careful. Certainly that does not help matters; and the helpers should themselves be Spirit-filled and grounded in the truth of God's Word. Again, these helpers must be humble, caring, and cautious.

Not only are we to restore the caught, but we are to restore the carnal. This person knows what he or she is doing, doesn't care who knows and have no plans to quit. James exhorts,

"My brethren, if any among you wanders from the truth, and someone turns him [or her] back, let him know that he who turns a sinner from the error of his [or her] way will save a soul from death and cover a multitude of sins" (James 5:19-20). Brackets are mine.

The person who is caught wants out, but the carnal person probably doesn't want out, nor does this person want to be bothered. In his conclusion James does not retract the hard words concerning those who go astray, but the possibility of turning both persons from error to the truth is held out.

Responsibility for this ministry of reconciliation is laid upon the *ordinary* Christian, not just upon the pastor. *"My brethren, if any among you wanders from the truth and someone brings [him or her] back ….."* In studying Church history you will notice there was no pronounced division between clergy and laity in those days, and the swift spread of the gospel and Christianity in the Roman world can largely be attributed to the fact that the humblest of Christians accepted the responsibility of witnessing the gospel among their pagan neighbors.

Those who found the *pearl of great price* enthusiastically told others about it without waiting for the pastor or other officer of the church to do it for them.

Jesus' parables of the lost sheep, the lost coin, the lost son, and His association with publicans and sinners – these all represent the pure genius of Christianity making it what it is. The state deals with the criminal with condemnation and punishment; the church sees him or her as a wandering brother or sister who must be redeemed. We need to shout it from the mountaintop – the Christian church is not:

* A social club with an exclusive membership.
* It is open to all on the sole terms of repentance.
* Neither is it simply an ethical culture for the *self*-improvement of its members.

The church is the reconciling agent of the kingdom which knows no boundaries; it is the servant of the abundant love of God which is for all peoples. He reconciled us to Himself and gave us the ministry of reconciliation (II Corinthians 5:18). Any church that does not function in this manner has forfeited its God-given purpose.

Too many Christians either lack faith to share with others or else lack the enthusiasm to share it. They are willing to leave the responsibility to the paid employees of the church. Many no longer believe that salvation is a matter of life and death. But can anyone look at the downward spiral of morals, fast-growing humanistic attitude, and "no God" philosophy invading the Christian community and not be affected by it? The majority of people in the world are traveling the *broad way* to destruction. The only choices before them are Christ's *narrow way* or destruction!

Encourage and buildup one another (1 Thessalonians 5:11; 4:17)

The goal of encouragement is to build other believers up. In v. 11, Paul admonishes the Thessalonian believers:

> *"Therefore comfort [encourage]*
> *each other*
> *and*
> *edify one another,*
> *just as you also are doing."*

What caused these Christians to crash and burn? Some of the people in the Thessalonian church had died, and the others were afraid they would never see them again. Paul stated that he wanted them to be informed, and also to be comforted by the *hope* of seeing their loved ones again. This was a hope their pagan neighbors did not have (see 4:13).

This hope (v. 13) for the departed Christians was as certain as the resurrection of Christ. Paul says that, *"God will bring with Him those who sleep in Jesus"* (v. 14). Many think this statement infers that departed Christians are unconscious until the Second Coming of Christ.

The Bible distinctly states in 2 Corinthians 5:8, "To be absent from the body and to be present with the Lord."

"For the Lord Himself will descend from heaven with a shout, with the voice of an archangel, and with the trumpet of God. And the dead in Christ will rise first. Then we who are alive and remain shall be caught up together with them in the clouds to meet the Lord in the air. And thus we shall always be with the Lord" (v. 17).

Therefore comfort one another with these words (v. 18). This sentence is in the present tense, indicating that it should be a constant comfort to us to think each day that the Lord may come.

Hopefully, all of us will realize the need for learning the Word of God, not just for ourselves. Romans 15:14 says,

*"Now I myself am confident concerning you, my brethren, that you also are full of goodness, filled with all knowledge, **and able also to admonish one another.**"*

As I stated in an earlier section, the church must take responsibility for training believers in "one another" ministries. God has given grace through the truths of His Word and our spiritual gifts assignments by the Holy Spirit (see Acts 1:8). God has entrusted with the ministry of hope, help, and healing people in the church – it encourages, builds up and brings hope!

I stated earlier, for any satisfactory accomplishment there must be proper preparation. By preparing, training, and focusing on the goal ahead, we can become fit to fight on to victory. Likewise, we must be holistically [spiritually, mentally, physically, and emotionally] engaged; if we are to be in shape and fit for the soon coming battle for truth brewing on the horizon in America's various culture and churches. Wake up America! Satan is rallying his satanic kingdom for an all-out offensive *against truth*; knowing that he has but a short time.

Count on Me

Is that your rallying cry? Can our Lord count on us? We know that those of us that live God's truth will be hated for speaking it. But we can't let that stop us from the work of the kingdom we are called to do. We are to represent Christ and His love in the world through speaking and defending His Word. We should not be discouraged by what we see around us and retreat into our comfortable four walls, disengaging ourselves from a world that so desperately *needs* to see the light.

I fully understand the discouragement that tries to pull us down. Sometimes when I look at the condition around us, especially in the churches I what to just sit down and cry. Things I would have never thought possible when I started out in the ministry forty four years ago are now considered normal. This is true both within the church and in the culture around us. Seeing these things can discourage the heart and make it difficult to keep moving forward and upward.

But it's in such a time as this, a time of extreme challenge that our training and preparation will pay off. We are admonished in Second Corinthians 2:14, *"Now thanks be to God who always leads us in triumph in Christ."* Do you trust Him? God will *always* lead His people into victory and triumph in Christ!

A message to the church, we must be fully prepared on every level and fully engaged, with our eyes fixed on the missions ahead – ready to bring in the harvest. We must lay aside all access baggage, even some people who would intentionally distract us – anything not essential to mission accomplishment.

In 1967-1968, I was in Vietnam. Some of you can remember and others probably heard about the Tet Offensive; which challenged America's politics from the Whitehouse to the battlefield. At a time when the nation was told daily of our successes on the battlefield and the enemy was easily being held at bay; We were hit by North Vietnam regulars along with the Viet Cong and probably every able-bodied sympathizer in South Vietnam. Of course we counter-attacked the next few days heavy fighting was on-going everything. I had no idea what day of the week it was, even losing sight of the month. My total focus was on the battle at hand and getting my troops through it. I lost one soldier in the initial attack to a rocket. Vietnam was a hotbed [everywhere] for the remainder of my tour. It was too late for planning and training drills, weapons familiarization, or warnings.

Our prior preparation and training brought us through; believe me after "day one" of the offensive every soldier in Vietnam at that time had been battle tested. But part of that preparation was making sure that my family was properly supplied with the resources needed to sustain them before I left the States. I could freely focus on the mission at hand. I often think of that Old Testament preacher named Noah, who preached and built an ark over a period of one hundred and twenty years. With instructions directly from God, I know he was focused on the mission at hand. He had one message. "It's going to rain!" That was his message for 120 years, and Noah acted upon it by faith "building an ark to the saving of his own family." I've heard some preachers say that he was not successful with only eight souls saved [his family] including himself. But before his mission began, notice what the Word of God in reference to Noah:

And God said to Noah, *"The end of all flesh has come before Me, for the earth is filled with violence through them;" and behold, "I will destroy them with the earth.* **Make yourself an ark** *of gopher-wood ...."* (Genesis 6:13-14).

"But Noah found **grace** *in the eyes of the Lord"* (Genesis 6:8).

"Noah was a **just** *man, perfect in his generations, Noah* **walked** *with God"* (Genesis 6:9).

"By faith Noah being divinely warned of things not yet seen, moved with **godly fear, prepared** *an ark* **for the saving of his household,** *by which he condemned the world and became heir of the righteousness which is according to* **faith**" (Hebrews 11:7).

Genesis 6:8 says, But Noah! Had there not been a man and a family who by the grace of God stood out from the wickedness of their day; there would have been a new beginning on the part of God that would have excluded all of us!

But Noah

The story of Noah and the building of the ark is much more than a story. It actually has postmodern parallels. There are many more arks needing to be built than Noah's. Noah was described as building the ark because there was a crisis at hand. Most people around him had no idea what was going on. And even if Noah warned them they only shrugged their shoulders and passed on by. This is generally what the majority of people will do today. Jesus said,

"In the days that were before the flood ...... they were eating and drinking, marrying and giving in marriage .... Until the flood came, and took them all away" (Matthew 24:38-39).

"Woe to them that are at ease in Zion" (Amos 6:1). This the prophet cried concerning the arrogant people of Israel which did not believe that their *destruction* by Assyria was coming – it was actually coming – in less than a generation. "I set watchmen over you," Jeremiah declared in the name of God, saying, *"Hearken to the sound of the trumpet."* But they said, *"We will not hearken"* (Jeremiah 6:17). No, not even when the Babylonians were already standing at their gates. *"My people are destroyed for lack of knowledge"* (Hosea 4:6). Like our society today, they were too engrossed with themselves to even want to know. When living according to Jesus' teachings; the Christian is a *constant unspoken condemnation* to the pagan's way of life.

Many times people stare so hard at what they want to see that the crucial realities are not seen. Jesus said, *"You know how to interpret the appearance of the sky, you cannot interpret the signs of the times"* (Matthew 16:3). The people of Noah's world looked at the ordinary skies that seemed to promise normal seasonal weather – but they did not see their downward spiral of moral facts and the immanent disaster. Since the middle of the twentieth century in America there has been an attitude and behavior similar to that of the people of Noah's day, they could eat and drink and rise up to play (see 1 Corinthians 10:7) thus, foreshadowing the coming judgment!

STUDY GUIDE: CHAPTER 14

1. A disciple is a _____ and a
   _____.

2. A church operating fully in the faith must be both _____
   and _____.

3. All disciples are expected to participate in _____
   _____ ministries.

4. 1 Corinthians 13 is called the _____.

5. What is the first "one another" ministry _____.

6. List 4 characteristics of love (1) (2) (3) (4)

7. The argument in Galatians 5:13 concerns _____ and
   _____.

8. "Overtaken" in sin means _____.

9. The Christian who willingly sin is _____.

10. The church is a _____ agent of the kingdom.

11. Christians who do not share their faith are lacking
    _____ or _____.

12. List two reasons why we should learn the Word:
    _____ and _____.

13. To meditate on the Word means to hide it in _____ your
    _____.

14. Prayerfully seek the Lord's _____ for your
    _____.

15. Christians are a constant _____ condemnation to
    the world.

NOTES

Dedication

1 *One Solitary Life,* Accessed 12/22/13 from http://www.holybible.com/resources/poems/ps.php?sid=47

Introduction

2 Charles Haddon Spurgeon, *The Metropolitan Pulpit, 1874,* p. 16: cited in *Spurgeon at His Best* (Grand Rapids: Baker, 1988), p. 102.

Chapter 1 Jesus is Lord

3 Robert E. Webber, Ancient-Future Faith 7th Printing (Baker Books Publishing 2006) 34-35

4 Bruce L. Shelly, *Church History in Plain Language* Third Edition (Zondervan Bible Publishers, 2008) 28

5 Ibid. 35

6 Ibid.

7 Ibid. 41

8 Ibid.

9 Ibid. Adapted from pages 43

10 Edited by Joshua Lingel, Jeff Morton, and Bill Nikides, *Chrislam* (12 Ministries Publishing 2011) 20

11 Shelly, Ibid. 45

12 Shelly, Ibid. 41

Chapter 2 Compromise Is A No No!

13 Accessed from Secular Humanism.

14 From *Spiritual Warfare in a Believer's Life* by Charles Spurgeon

Chapter 3 Warm and Model Christians

15 Kevin J. Conner, The Foundations of Christian Doctrine (Bible Press 1980) 104

16 Ibid 105

17 William J. Federer, *Change to Chains* (Amerisearch, St. Louis, MO, 2011) 57

18 Ibid,

19 Ibid. 61

20 Ibid.

21 Ibid. 150

Chapter 4 The Narrow Way

22 Ibid. William J. Federer

23 Harry R. Jackson Jr. & Tony Perkins, *Personal Faith-Public Policy* (Frontline Pub. 2008) Page 155

24 Accessed on January 18, 2014, from Inovative Media Inc. and Christianity Today.

25 Ibid.

26 Edward Gibbon, [Edited by J. B. Bury]*The Decline and Fall of the Roman Empire Vol. 1* (Wildside Press 2004) 285

27 Arnold Toynbee, *A Study of History Vol. 1-3* (Oxford University 1961)

28 Adrian Goldsby, *How Rome Fell: Death of a Superpower* (Yale University Press 2009) 80

29 Adapted from subtopic God's Wise Attitude: Kyle Searcy, *The Secret of Biblical Wisdom* (Chosen Books, 2012) 101

Chapter 6 To Be or Not To Be

30 Alfred P. Gibbs, Worship: The Christian's Highest Occupation (Walterick Publishers 2013) 207

31 Ibid.

32 Jay R. Leach, *How Should We Then Live* (iUniverse Publishers 2010) 52

33 Ibid.

34 Ibid.

Chapter 8 Community – The Narrow Way

35 Robert E. Webber, Ancient-Future Faith (Published by Baker Books 2006) 78

36 Ibid.

37 Ibid.

38 Ibid.

39 W. E. Vine's Greek Grammar and Dictionary (Thomas Nelson Publishers 2012) 294

Chapter 9 Guidance – The Narrow Way

[40] Larry Richards, *The Smart Guide to the Bible* (Nelson Reference, a Division of Thomas Nelson, Inc 2006) Adapted from pages 234-235

[41] Dr. Warren Wiersbe, *Expository Outlines on the New Testament* Chariot Victor Publishing 1992) pages 98-90

[42] Ibid.

Chapter 10 Godliness – The Narrow Way

[43] Dr. Mark Brewer, What's Your Spiritual Quotient? (Destiny Image Publishers Inc 2008) Adapted from pages 48-51

[44] Ibid.

[45] Ibid.

Chapter 11 Re-Thinking Church

[46] "The Year's Most Intriguing Findings," Barna Research Online, December 17, 2001, http://www.barna.org, 2.

[47] Ibid.

[48] Aubrey Malphurs, *A New Kind of Church* (Baker Books Publishing 2007) Adapted from pages 30-33

[49] Ibid.

[50] Ibid.

[51] Ibid.

[52] Ibid.

[53] http://www.barna.org/.org/barna-update/culture/661-americans-divided-on-the-importance-of-c... Accessed 4/4/2014.

[54] Ibid.

[55] Ibid.

[56] Ibid.

[57] Ibid.

[58] Graham Johnson, *Preaching to a Postmodern World* (Baker Books 2004) adapted from pages 88-91

[59] Ibid. 26

Chapter 12 Yes We Can

[60] Oscar E. Feucht, Everyone a Minster (Jove Publications Inc. 2001) pages 35-38
Chapter 14 Forward and Upward

[61] Jay R. Leach, A Light Unto My Path (Trafford Publishing 2013) pages 96-101